TEACHER'S PET PUBLICATIONS

LITPLAN TEACHER PACK
for
A Christmas Carol
based on the book by
Charles Dickens

Written by
Barbara M. Linde, MA Ed.

© 1996 Teacher's Pet Publications
All Rights Reserved

This **LitPlan** on Charles Dickens' **A Christmas Carol** has been brought to you by Teacher's Pet Publications, Inc.

Copyright Teacher's Pet Publications 1996

Only the student materials in this unit plan may be reproduced. Pages such as worksheets and study guides may be reproduced for use in the purchaser's classroom. For any additional copyright questions, contact Teacher's Pet Publications.

www.tpet.com

TABLE OF CONTENTS - *A Christmas Carol*

Introduction	9
Unit Objectives	11
Unit Outline	12
Reading Assignment Sheet	13
Study Questions	17
Quiz/Study Questions (multiple choice)	26
Pre-reading Vocabulary Worksheets	43
Lesson One (Introductory Lesson)	67
Writing Assignment 1	74
Nonfiction Assignment Sheet	75
Writing Evaluation Form	76
Oral Reading Evaluation Form	79
Writing Assignment 2	86
Extra Writing Assignments/Discussion ?s	91
Vocabulary Review Activities	98
Unit Review Activities	99
Writing Assignment	104
Unit Tests	109
Unit Resource Materials	145
Vocabulary Resource Materials	161

A FEW NOTES ABOUT THE AUTHOR
CHARLES DICKENS

DICKENS, Charles (1812-70). On a pier in New York Harbor in 1841 a crowd watched a tall sailing ship from England being towed to the pierhead. There was no ocean communication cable as yet and the ship brought the latest news. A question was yelled from the pier to the ship: "Is Little Nell dead?" Little Nell was the heroine in a serial called 'Old Curiosity Shop'. The latest installment was on the ship, and the people were anxious to learn how the story came out.

The author who could stir people to such excitement was Charles Dickens, then a young man of 29. The next year, on his visit to America, he received a reception second only to that of Lafayette in 1824. Six years before, with his 'Pickwick Papers', he had become the world's most celebrated writer.

Charles Dickens was born on Feb. 7, 1812, in Portsmouth. His father, John Dickens, was a minor clerk in the navy offices, a friendly man with a large family (Charles was the second of eight children) and only a moderate income. The family drifted from one poor home in London to another, each shabbier than the last. Presently John Dickens ended up in the Marshalsea Prison for debt and took his wife and younger children with him.

Meanwhile young Charles worked in a ramshackle warehouse, lived in a garret, visited his family in prison on Sundays, and felt that his life was shattered before it had begun. For a fictionalized account of his early life, read 'David Copperfield'. Then a timely inheritance restored the family to something like comfortable means, and Charles had a few quiet years at a private school.

Later he immortalized his father, for whom he always had a great love, as Mr. Micawber. When his own rising fortune and fame gave him control of a great newspaper, he put his father on the staff to preside over the dispatches and bought him a small country house. Dickens' mother, unsympathetic and unconscious of his genius, meant less to him; she begrudged his leaving work to go to school. He made her immortal as Mrs. Nickleby.

Dickens made his own career. A few years of secondary school was his basic education. He never attended college. His real education came from his reading and observation and daily experience. Except for the English novels of the 18th century, he knew little of great literature. Of history and foreign politics, he knew practically nothing. His novels all deal with his own day and his own environment, except for his two historical novels-'A Tale of Two Cities' and 'Barnaby Rudge'-and these were set in the recent past of the French Revolution and the Gordon Riots.

The qualities that made up Dickens' genius did not depend on formal education for development. Dickens had a reporter's eye for the details of daily life and a mimic's ear for the subtleties of common speech. Further, he had the artist's ability to select what he needed
from these raw materials of observation and to shape them into works of enduring merit.

Preparation for a Career

By teaching himself shorthand, Dickens secured the position of court reporter in the old Doctors' Commons, a survival from Elizabethan days that handled marriage, divorce, wills, and other "ghostly" causes. This experience gave Dickens a peculiar dislike of law that never left him; forever after it seemed either comic as in "Bardell vs. Pickwick" or terrible with tragedy as in 'Bleak House'. Dickens moved up in 1831 to the Reporters' Gallery of the "old-the unburned and unreformed-House of Commons." He also went to other cities and towns to report election speeches, transcribing his notes on the palm of his hand "by the light of a dark lantern in a post-chaise and four." This experience gave him a detailed and sometimes cynical view of government. To him the voters were often represented by the Eatanswill Election in 'Pickwick', parliamentary government by Doodle and Foodle and Coodle ('Our Mutual Friend'), and civil service by the Circumlocution Office ('Little Dorrit').

Thus equipped, Charles Dickens set out to conquer the world. The stage was his first dream. Night after night for two or three years he sat entranced with the melodrama of the London theaters-lurid with love, battle, treachery, and blue fire, in which a heroic young man would knock over 16 smugglers like ninepins. Melodrama put a stamp on Dickens for life. His characters, if they get excited, drop into the ranting language of the old Adelphi Theatre. On the other hand, Dickens' intense concentration on acting helped to give him that weird, almost hypnotic, power that he showed in the public reading of his works.

However, fate led him to a different career. He had a passion for creative writing, and he has told of his great joy, of his eyes dimmed with tears when a manuscript sent anonymously to an editor appeared in print. So he began writing sketches under the name of "Boz," the family nickname of a younger brother. To "Boz" came sudden and great success. The publishers, Chapman and Hall, had a plan for some serial pictures of cockney sportsmen, a Nimrod club, having all sorts of misadventures. The humor of the period turned very much on such horseplay. An artist named Seymour had drawn one or two pictures. They asked young "Boz" to write a set of stories to go with the pictures. Knowing nothing of sport, Dickens suggested changing the activities of the Nimrod club from sport to travel. When the publishers agreed, then, says Dickens, "I thought of Mr. Pickwick," which is all that has ever been known of the origin and genesis of one of the greatest characters in humorous literature. The young author was to receive 14 guineas (about $70) for each monthly installment.

The very week that the 'Pickwick Papers' began their monthly appearance, in April 1836, Dickens married Catherine Hogarth, one of the three pretty daughters of a newspaper associate. The young couple moved into rooms in Furnival's Inn. They did not realize that one day they would separate with bitter words because they believed they had made a love match. Dickens looked on Catherine, beautiful and silent, and saw nothing but the reflection of himself. Catherine looked at Charles and did not realize that genius and egotism often lie close together. Dickens indeed was not so much in love with Catherine as in love with love.

At first the 'Pickwick Papers' failed to sell more than a few hundred copies a month. Then the serial introduced the character of Mr. Sam Weller, polishing boots at the White Hart Inn. The narrative took off on the wings of imagination, down English lanes, past gabled inns, and along the highways as varied and as cheery as a flying coach at a gallop, and the world was at the author's feet. The phenomenal 'Pickwick

Papers' and the books that followed steadily lifted young "Boz" to the height of success, from poverty to wealth, from obscurity to fame, all in a few brief years. The great novels of this period were 'Oliver Twist' (published in 1838), 'Nicholas Nickleby' (1839), 'Old Curiosity Shop' (1841), and 'Barnaby Rudge' (1841).

Dickens in America

Dickens now looked around for other worlds to conquer. America had welcomed his books from the start, in part because the lack of international copyright permitted American publishers to print them without paying him. Dickens, in his youth a radical who hated Toryism and aristocracy, longed to study America and its freedom at first hand. Leaving their four children at home, he landed with his wife in Boston in January 1842. The town blazed with excitement; society was thrilled; there were dinners, receptions, adulation. Young Dickens, dressed in a bright velvet waistcoat, reveled in his new and adoring audience and wrote home of the freedom of America and the comforts of the workers. H.W. Longfellow, William Ellery Channing, and others of the New England elite joined in the welcome. Young Dr. Oliver Wendell Holmes was one of those who helped to organize it.

Dickens found in Boston friendships that he never lost, even when bitterness and disillusion altered his view of America. From Boston he went to New York and a "Boz" ball of 3,000 people; to Philadelphia and a huge public reception; then to Baltimore and to Washington, where he met President John Tyler and the Congress; then to Richmond, which offered him a taste of Southern culture. Such was the triumphant progress of the young author, only a few years before a member of the shabby-genteel class of London.

Always ready to raise his voice in defense of a cause he believed in, Dickens spoke everywhere of the need for an international copyright agreement that would protect the rights of both American and British writers. He felt that it was unfair and unjust that American publishers should print and sell his books without permission from him and without paying him any royalties. Dickens did not speak of himself as the sole victim of this practice. He pointed out that all British authors were equally victimized; he also acknowledged that American authors, such as Edgar Allan Poe, suffered from the pirating of their works in England.

The newspapers in America attacked these forthright statements and accused Dickens of bad taste and of abusing American hospitality. In time Dickens' rosy view of America faded. The proof of his disillusion and disgust is revealed in his 'American Notes' (published in 1842), his letters to friends, and 'Martin Chuzzlewit' (1844). From Dickens' viewpoint, Americans all seemed to chew tobacco. They kept slaves, whom he never stopped to compare with the factory slaves of England. American government seemed all plunder and roguery. Then he went West, traveling as far as Cairo, Ill. His vision of the West contained nothing but foul and reeking canal boats, swamps, bullfrogs, and tobacco juice.

Dickens lacked the eye to see the pageant of America, the great epic of the settlements of the West; the eye to compare the canal boat with the raft and the scow of earlier settlers. He became peevish, impatient of small discomforts, resenting the fact that hotelkeepers dared to talk to him. He spent two weeks in Canada, consoled there by the presence of friends at the English garrison in Montreal. Then he returned home to discredit America with his pen.

Fame and Fortune

The years that followed Dickens' return from America-the middle period of his life-were filled with more activity, fame, and success. In 1851 he took a fine residence at Tavistock Square and lived in great style. His friends were the leading authors, artists, and actors of the day. Later on, his purchase of a country house at Gad's Hill fulfilled an ambition of his childhood. His books, appearing in monthly serial parts, enjoyed a popularity that slackened only to rise again. It is generally thought that 'David Copperfield', written as a serial in 1848 and 1849, when he was at the height of his powers, is the greatest of his novels. Contrasted with the 'Pickwick Papers', it shows the transition of Dickens' genius from the exuberance of youth to the somber acceptance of middle age.

One of his books, 'Dombey and Son', is a sort of epic of great sorrow. Dickens' books indeed appealed to his generation of readers as much for their tears as for their laughter.

Reformer-Journalist

Book writing did not entirely satisfy Dickens' ego. The onetime reporter wanted to be a newspaper editor. Dickens felt the need to reform all England. The way to do it, he felt, was to control and edit a great daily newspaper, where he should preside like Jupiter handing out lightning. Enthusiastic friends subscribed £100,000 and founded the Daily News. In January 1846 Dickens threw himself eagerly into the editorial chair of the fledgling publication and threw himself out again in 19 days. He found that in the newspaper business the lightning hits in two directions. So in 1850 he founded instead a weekly journal, Household Words, and carried on with it and a later magazine, All the Year Round (1859), until his death. Several of his own stories, 'Christmas Stories', 'A Tale of Two Cities', 'Great Expectations', and others ran in his magazine.

Dickens as Actor and Lecturer

Another activity, and this a special delight to him, was amateur theatricals that carried on Dickens' love of the stage. He himself had incomparable dramatic power. With it he had a great talent for management and an energy and enthusiasm that carried all before it. On May 16, 1851, at a performance that was given at the duke of Devonshire's London house for a charity, the young Queen Victoria and her Prince Consort and the duke of Wellington were in the audience. The queen came to a later performance in 1857 and graciously "commanded Mr. Dickens' presence"-an invitation of great honor-after the show. Mr. Dickens being in "farce" dress asked to be excused from appearing, thus defying all royal precedents.

To theatricals he soon added public lectures and readings from his works. This activity began after he had read one of his famous Christmas stories to a group of friends who received it enthusiastically. He made a number of successful tours in England, Scotland, and Ireland-from 1858 to 1859, 1861 to 1863, 1866 to 1867, and 1869 to 1870.

Relief in Work

Dickens separated from his wife in 1858. Georgina Hogarth, his wife's younger sister, had lived with the couple since 1842. She remained with Dickens until his death. His will provided for both women.

Dickens sought relief from a public curious about his personal life in the excitement of work. He made a second American tour in 1867 to 1868. It was an overwhelming success but extremely fatiguing. At home again, he resumed lecturing. His last appearance was in March 1870.

In retirement he struggled with his last task, 'The Mystery of Edwin Drood', a tale of night and storm and murder. The book was still unfinished on June 9, 1870, when Dickens died.

In the opinion of many, Dickens is England's greatest creative writer. The names and natures of his characters are unforgettable. His humor is unsurpassable, not only in the laughter that lies on the surface, but in the warmth of human kindliness below. His books are still being read all over the world. 'A Christmas Carol', conceived and written in a few weeks in 1843, is the ultimate, enduring Christmas myth of modern literature.

--- Courtesy of Compton's Learning Company

INTRODUCTION

This unit has been designed to develop students' reading, writing, thinking, listening and speaking skills through exercises and activities related to *A Christmas Carol* by Charles Dickens. It includes twenty lessons, supported by extra resource materials.

The **introductory lesson** introduces students to one main theme of the novel, sharing with others, through a bulletin board activity. Following the introductory activity, students are given an explanation of how the activity relates to the book they are about to read.

The **reading assignments** are approximately twenty-five pages each; some are a little shorter while others are a little longer. Students have approximately 15 minutes of pre-reading work to do prior to each reading assignment. This pre-reading work involves reviewing the study questions for the assignment and doing some vocabulary work for 8 to 10 vocabulary words they will encounter in their reading.

The **study guide questions** are fact-based questions; students can find the answers to these questions right in the text. These questions come in two formats: short answer or multiple choice. The best use of these materials is probably to use the short answer version of the questions as study guides for students (since answers will be more complete), and to use the multiple choice version for occasional quizzes. It might be a good idea to make transparencies of your answer keys for the overhead projector.

The **vocabulary work** is intended to enrich students' vocabularies as well as to aid in the students' understanding of the book. Prior to each reading assignment, students will complete a two-part worksheet for 10 vocabulary words in the upcoming reading assignment. Part I focuses on students' use of general knowledge and contextual clues by giving the sentence in which the word appears in the text. Students are then to write down what they think the words mean based on the words' usage. Part II gives students dictionary definitions of the words and has them match the words to the correct definitions based on the words' contextual usage. Students should then have an understanding of the words when they meet them in the text. Due to the heavy vocabulary load in *A Christmas Carol*, an extra vocabulary section has been added. Potentially difficult words, and their definitions, are listed as a resource for the teacher. These words are not tested.

After each reading assignment, students will go back and formulate answers for the study guide questions. Discussion of these questions serves as a **review** of the most important events and ideas presented in the reading assignments.

After students complete extra discussion questions, there is a **vocabulary review** lesson which pulls together all of the separate vocabulary lists for the reading assignments and gives students a review of all of the words they have studied.

Following the reading of the book, two lessons are devoted to the **extra discussion questions/writing**

assignments. These questions focus on interpretation, critical analysis and personal response, employing a variety of thinking skills and adding to the students' understanding of the novel. These questions are done as a **group activity**. Using the information they have acquired so far through individual work and class discussions, students get together to further examine the text and to brainstorm ideas relating to the themes of the novel.

The group activity is followed by a **reports and discussion** session in which the groups share their ideas about the book with the entire class; thus, the entire class gets exposed to many different ideas regarding the themes and events of the book.

There are three **writing assignments** in this unit, each with the purpose of informing, persuading, or having students express personal opinions. The first assignment is to **inform: students** will research a topic and write a report about it. The second assignment is to **persuade**: students will write a letter requesting that someone support a cause they are sponsoring. The third assignment is to express a personal **opinion**: students will give their opinion of the meaning of the holiday spirit.

Writing assignment #1 is used as the **nonfiction reading assignment**. Students are required to read a piece of nonfiction related in some way to *A Christmas Carol*. After reading their nonfiction pieces, students will fill out a worksheet on which they answer questions regarding facts, interpretation, criticism, and personal opinions. They will also write a detailed report about the topic. During one class period, students make **oral presentations** about the nonfiction pieces they have read. This not only exposes all students to a wealth of information, it also gives students the opportunity to practice **public speaking**.

The **review lesson** pulls together all of the aspects of the unit. The teacher is given four or five choices of activities or games to use which all serve the same basic function of reviewing all of the information presented in the unit.

The **unit test** comes in two formats: all multiple choice-matching-true/false or with a mixture of matching, short answer, and composition. As a convenience, two different tests for each format have been included.

There are additional **support materials** included with this unit. The **unit resource section** includes suggestions for an in-class library, crossword and word search puzzles related to the novel, and extra vocabulary worksheets. There is a list of **bulletin board ideas** which gives the teacher suggestions for bulletin boards to go along with this unit. In addition, there is a list of **extra class activities** the teacher could choose from to enhance the unit or as a substitution for an exercise the teacher might feel is inappropriate for his/her class. **Answer keys** are located directly after the **reproducible student materials** throughout the unit. The student materials may be reproduced for use in the teacher's classroom without infringement of copyrights. No other portion of this unit may be reproduced without the written consent of Teacher's Pet Publications, Inc.

UNIT OBJECTIVES *A Christmas Carol*

1. Through reading *A Christmas Carol* students will analyze characters and their situations to better understand the themes of the novel.

2. Students will demonstrate their understanding of the text on four levels: factual, interpretive, critical, and personal.

3. Students will practice reading aloud and silently to improve their skills in each area.

4. Students will enrich their vocabularies and improve their understanding of the novel through the vocabulary lessons prepared for use in conjunction with it.

5. Students will identify the differences between the British and American spelling of selected words from the novel.

6. Students will answer questions to demonstrate their knowledge and understanding of the main events and characters in *A Christmas Carol*.

7. Students will practice writing through a variety of writing assignments.

8. The writing assignments in this are geared to several purposes:
    a. To check the students' reading comprehension
    b. To make students think about the ideas presented by the novel
    c. To make students put those ideas into perspective
    d. To encourage critical and logical thinking
    e. To provide the opportunity to practice good grammar and improve students' use of the English language.

9. Students will read aloud, report, and participate in large and small group discussions to improve their public speaking and personal interaction skills.

10. Students will use text, visual media, and online resources to research a non-fiction topic related to the novel.

UNIT OUTLINE *A Christmas Carol*

1 Unit Intro Distribute Unit Materials Project Tiny Tim	2 PVR Stave 1	3 Study ?? Stave 1 Non-Fiction/Writing Assignment 1	4 PVR Stave 2 Oral Reading Evaluation	5 Study ?? Stave 2 Minilesson: Story Map
6 PVR Stave 3	7 Study ?? Stave 3 Minilesson: British Spellings	8 Writing Assignment #2	9 PVR 4	10 Writing Conferences
11 Study ?? Stave 4 Minilesson: Adjectives	12 PVR Stave 5 Study ?? Stave 5	13 Extra Discussion ??	14 Vocabulary Review	15 Unit Review
16 Test	17 Non-Fiction Assignment	18 Writing Assignment #3	19 Movie/ Audio Cassette and Discussion	20 Project

Key: P = Preview Study Questions   V = Vocabulary Work   R = Read

READING ASSIGNMENT SHEET
A Christmas Carol

Date to be Assigned	Chapters	Completion Date
	Stave 1 Marley's Ghost	
	Stave 2 The First of the Three Spirits	
	Stave 3 The Second of the Three Spirits	
	Stave 4 The Last of the Sprits	
	Stave 5 The End of It	

STUDY QUESTIONS

SHORT ANSWER STUDY QUESTIONS *A Christmas Carol*

Stave 1 Marley's Ghost

1. Who was Marley? What was his condition at the beginning of the story?
2. What is the setting of the story?
3. One of Scrooge's relatives visited him at his warehouse. Who was it, and what did he want? What was Scrooge's reply?
4. What did the other men who came to the warehouse want? What was Scrooge's reply to them?
5. What did Scrooge say about giving his clerk a day off to celebrate Christmas?
6. What happened to the door knocker when Scrooge was opening his door?
7. Who appeared to Scrooge? What did he tell Scrooge?
8. This visitor told Scrooge about some other visitors who would be coming. Who were they? When would they come?
9. What did Scrooge do after his visitor left?

Stave Two The First of the Three Spirits

1. What did Scrooge notice about the church chimes when he woke up? What did he think had happened?
2. Describe what the first Spirit looked like. Who was the first Spirit? What was its purpose?
3. Scrooge asked the Spirit what business brought him there. What was the Spirit's answer?
4. Describe the first scene Scrooge and the Spirit visited. How did Scrooge feel about what he saw?
5. Who was Fan? Describe the scene with her.
6. Describe the scene at Fezziwig's warehouse. What did Scrooge say to the Ghost about the scene?
7. Describe the scenes with Belle.
8. How did Scrooge try to get rid of the Ghost? What happened?

Stave Three The Second of the Three Spirits

1. How did Scrooge find the second Spirit?
2. Describe the scene when Scrooge found the second Spirit.
3. Who was the second Spirit? Describe him.
4. Describe the first place they went.
5. What was the second place they visited?
6. Who was Tiny Tim? What did Scrooge ask the Ghost about Tiny Tim? What was the Ghost's reply?
7. Describe the Cratchit family's toast to Scrooge.
8. What were some of the other places the Ghost took Scrooge? What did Scrooge find at each place?
9. What did Scrooge's nephew and nieces say about him?
10. What did Scrooge think about when he heard the harp music?
11. What did Scrooge do while his nephew and the others were playing games?
12. Describe the "Yes and No" game. What was the subject of the game?

13. How did Scrooge feel by the time he and the Spirit left his nephew's house?
14. What happened to the way the Ghost and Scrooge looked as the night went on?
15. Who were the two children the Ghost had under its robe? What did the Spirit tell Scrooge about them?
16. What was the Spirit's reply to Scrooge's question: "Have they no refuge or resource?"

Stave 4 The Last of the Spirits
1. How did Scrooge feel about the Ghost of Christmas Yet to Come?
2. What did the Ghost of Christmas Yet to Come look like?
3. Where did Scrooge and the Spirit go first?
4. What were the business men talking about?
5. What was Scrooge's attitude about being with the third Spirit?
6. Where did they go second? What did they see?
7. What was Scrooge's reaction to the scene?
8. What did Scrooge think about when he saw the dead man?
9. Scrooge asked the Spirit to show him someone who felt emotion at the man's death. Describe the person the Spirit showed him.
10. What did Scrooge ask the Ghost to show him next? What did the Ghost show him?
11. Who had been kind to Bob Cratchit, and what was the kindness?
12. Who was the dead man? How did Scrooge discover who it was?
13. What question did Scrooge ask the Ghost as they stood among the graves?
14. What did Scrooge tell the Ghost he would do?

Stave 5 The End of It
1. Describe Scrooge's behavior when he woke up.
2. What day was it when Scrooge woke up?
3. What did Scrooge ask the boy under his window to do, and why?
4. How did Scrooge act when he went outside?
5. What did Scrooge do when he met the man who had asked for a donation the day before?
6. Whom did Scrooge visit? What was the reaction?
7. What happened at the office the next morning?
8. How did Scrooge spend the rest of his life?

ANSWER KEY: SHORT ANSWER STUDY QUESTIONS *A Christmas Carol*

Stave 1 Marley's Ghost

1. Who was Marley? What was his condition at the beginning of the story?
   Marley was Ebenezer Scrooge's business partner. He had been dead for seven years when the story opened.

2. What is the setting of the story?
   It takes place on Christmas Eve and Christmas Day in London. The year is not given.

3. One of Scrooge's relatives visited him at his warehouse. Who was it, and what did he want? What was Scrooge's reply?
   Scrooge's nephew came to wish him a merry Christmas and invite him for Christmas dinner. Scrooge said he did not think keeping Christmas had ever helped his nephew. He asked the nephew why he had married. He replied only "Good Afternoon" when the nephew invited Scrooge to dinner.

4. What did the other men who came to the warehouse want? What was Scrooge's reply to them?
   They asked for a donation for the poor and destitute. Scrooge replied that he did not make merry, and could not afford to help idle people make merry.

5. What did Scrooge say about giving his clerk a day off to celebrate Christmas?
   He thought it was unfair that he should pay the man a day's wages for a day he was not working. He was also annoyed that the clerk wanted the whole day off.

6. What happened to the door knocker when Scrooge was opening his door?
   It turned into Jacob Marley's face, then back to a door knocker.

7. Who appeared to Scrooge? What did he tell Scrooge?
   Marley's ghost appeared. He told Scrooge he was doomed to travel the world forever and look at all of the kindness and happiness he had missed. The chains he wore were ones he had made himself when he was alive. He said Scrooge was headed on the same path, and had a chain even longer than his own. He also said Scrooge still had a chance to redeem himself.

8. This visitor told Scrooge about some other visitors who would be coming. Who were they? When would they come?
   Three Spirits were to come, one each night for the next three nights.

9. What did Scrooge do after his visitor left?
   At first he saw more phantoms when he looked out the window. Then he closed the window and went to sleep.

Stave Two The First of the Three Spirits

1. What did Scrooge notice about the church chimes when he woke up? What did he think had happened?
   The chimes went from six all the way to twelve, then stopped. It had been past two when Scrooge went to bed, so he thought the clock was wrong. Then he wondered if he had slept through an entire day. He wondered if something had happened to the sun and it was really noon. The more he thought, the more puzzled he became.

2. Describe the first Spirit. What was it called?
   It was like a child and an old man at the same time. It had long white hair and a face without wrinkles. Its arms and legs were long and strong. The Spirit wore a white tunic trimmed with summer flowers. Its belt sparkled and glimmered in different parts. There was a jet of light coming from the crown of its head. It held a branch of green holly in one hand. It was the Ghost of Christmas Past.

3. Scrooge asked the Spirit what business brought him there. What was the Spirit's answer?
   It said Scrooge's welfare and reclamation brought it.

4. Describe the first scene Scrooge and the Spirit visited. How did Scrooge feel abut what he saw?
   It was Scrooge's boyhood home and school. They saw Scrooge as a young boy, reading. At first Scrooge seemed excited. Then he seemed to pity his former self. After that he said he wished he had given something to the young boy who had been singing at his door the night before.

5. Who was Fan? Describe the scene with her.
   Fan was Scrooge's younger sister. She came to the school to get him, saying their father had agreed that he could come home. The Ghost commented that she had died as an adult, but had children. Scrooge replied that she had one child. The Spirit reminded Scrooge this was his nephew.

6. Describe the scene at Fezziwig's warehouse. What did Scrooge say to the Ghost about the scene?
   Fezziwig was Scrooge's former master. He was hosting a Christmas party for his family and his employees. He danced with his wife. After watching it, Scrooge said that Fezziwig had the power to make the others happy or unhappy. Scrooge said he wished he could talk to his clerk then.

7. Describe the scenes with Belle.
   Belle was a young woman to whom Scrooge was apparently engaged. She told him she was releasing him from his promise to marry her. She felt that money and gain were more important to him than she was. Later Scrooge saw her with her husband and family. Her husband mentioned that he had seen Scrooge sitting alone in his office. At that point, Scrooge asked the Ghost to take him away.

8. How did Scrooge try to get rid of the Ghost? What happened?
   Scrooge took the extinguisher-cap and pressed it down on the Ghost's head. The Spirit dropped under the hat, but the light still shone. Scrooge realized he was in his own bedroom. He fell on the bed and went to sleep.

Stave Three The Second of the Three Spirits

1. How did Scrooge find the second Spirit?
   Scrooge was waiting in his bed when the hour struck, but nothing happened. Then Scrooge noticed a blaze of light, and thought it was coming from the adjoining room. He opened the door and found the Spirit in there.

2. Describe the scene when Scrooge found the second Spirit.
   They were in Scrooge's room, but the room was decorated with holly, mistletoe, and ivy. There was a large fire in the fireplace. Delicious foods were in abundance.

3. Who was the second Spirit? Describe it.
   It was the Ghost of Christmas Present. It wore a green robe with a white fur border. It had bare feet, and wore a holly wreath over its long, brown curls.

4. Describe the first place they went.
   They went to the streets on Christmas morning. Scrooge saw people shoveling snow. He saw all of the food in the grocery shops. Then he saw people carrying their dinners to the bakers. The Spirit sprinkled some kind of water on people who began quarreling with each other.

5. What was the second place they visited?
   They visited the home of Scrooge's clerk, Bob Cratchit. The Cratchit family members were celebrating, even though they didn't have much material wealth.

6. Who was Tiny Tim? What did Scrooge ask the Ghost about Tiny Tim? What was the Ghost's reply?
   Tiny Tim was the Cratchits' youngest son. He was sickly and lame. Scrooge wanted to know if Tiny Tim would live or die. The Ghost replied that if things did not change in the future, Tiny Tim would die.

7. Describe the Cratchit family's toast to Scrooge.
    Bob Cratchit offered a toast to Scrooge, calling him "The Founder of the Feast." Mrs. Cratchit did not want to drink to his health, saying he was odious and stingy. Bob asked her to do so in the spirit of Christmas, and she did. The children also drank a toast, but did not enjoy it. Tiny Tim said, "God bless us, everyone."

8. What were some of the other places the Ghost took Scrooge? What did Scrooge find at each place?
    The Ghost took Scrooge to a miner's camp, a lighthouse, and a ship. Scrooge saw that the people at each location were happily celebrating Christmas.

9. What did Scrooge's nephew and nieces say about him?
    His nephew thought Scrooge was a "comical old fellow." He said he felt sorry for Scrooge, that he was the one who really suffered for his own ill whims. Scrooge's niece and the other women said they had no patience with him.

10. What did Scrooge think about when he heard the harp music?
    He thought that if he could have listened to it more when he was younger, he might have been able to be kinder.

11. What did Scrooge do while his nephew and the others were playing games?
    He joined in, even though they couldn't see or hear him.

12. Describe the "Yes and No" game. What was the subject of the game?
    Scrooge's nephew thought of something, and the rest had to find out what it was by asking questions that could be answered either "yes" or "no." Clues were that it was a live, disagreeable animal that lived in London. One of the nieces guessed that it was Scrooge.

13. How did Scrooge feel by the time he and the Spirit left his nephew's house?
    He was cheerful and light-hearted. He thanked them, although his thanks was not heard.

14. What happened to the way the Ghost and Scrooge looked as the night went on?
    Scrooge stayed the same but the Ghost got older.

15. Who were the two children the Ghost had under its robe? What did the Spirit tell Scrooge about them?
    The boy was Ignorance, and the girl was Want. The Spirit warned Scrooge to beware of both of them, but especially the boy. Doom was written on his forehead, and would stay there unless it could be erased.

16. What was the Spirit's reply to Scrooge's question: "Have they no refuge or resource?"
    The Spirit replied with Scrooge's own early response: "Are there no prisons? Are there no workhouses?"

Stave 4 The Last of the Spirits
1. How did Scrooge feel about the Ghost of Christmas Yet to Come?
    He feared this Ghost. His legs trembled, and he could hardly stand up.

2. What did the Ghost of Christmas Yet to Come look like?
    It was covered by a black garment. It was tall, and did not speak.

3. Where did Scrooge and the Spirit go first?
    They went to the city.

4. What were the business men talking about?
    They were discussing another businessman's (Old Scratch) death and what he had done with his money. They also wondered who would go to his funeral, since none of them liked him and he had no friends.

5. What was Scrooge's attitude about being with the third Spirit?
    He knew he would learn something for his own improvement. He treasured everything he heard and saw.

6. Where did they go second? What did they see?
    The Spirit took Scrooge to an obscure part of town. They saw two men and two women; an old man (Joe), an undertaker's assistant, a charwoman, and a laundress (Mrs. Dilber.) They all had bundles that they had taken from the dead man Scrooge had seen earlier.

7. What was Scrooge's reaction to the scene?
    He reacted with horror and disgust. He realized it might be his own unhappy end.

8. What did Scrooge think about when he saw the dead man?
    He wondered what the man's thoughts would be if he were alive. He thought that avarice and hard dealing had caused an early death.

9. Scrooge asked the Spirit to show him someone who felt emotion at the man's death. Describe the person the Spirit showed him.
    It was a man who owed money to the dead man. He and his wife were glad the lender was dead because they thought another creditor would have more mercy on them.

10. What did Scrooge ask the Ghost to show him next? What did the Ghost show him?
    Scrooge asked the Ghost to show him some tenderness connected with a death. The Ghost took him to the Cratchit home, where they were mourning the death of Tiny Tim.

11. Who had been kind to Bob Cratchit, and what was the kindness?
    Scrooge's nephew offered sympathy about Tiny Tim. Bob Cratchit thought he might also get a better situation for Peter.

12. Who was the dead man? How did Scrooge discover who it was?
    He asked the Ghost to tell him. The Ghost took him to his house, but another man was living there. Then the Ghost took him to the graveyard where Scrooge read his name on the head stone.

13. What question did Scrooge ask the Ghost as they stood among the graves?
    He asked if the shadow were of things that Will be or May be.

14. What did Scrooge tell the Ghost he would do?
    He promised to honor Christmas and keep it all year. He said the Spirits of Past, Present, and Future would work within him.

<u>Stave 5 The End of It</u>
1. Describe Scrooge's behavior when he woke up.
    He was excited, laughing and crying at the same time. When he saw that the bed curtains were still up, he said he was encouraged that the sad things he had seen could change. He looked around the room for familiar items to convince himself the visits by the Spirits had really happened.

2. What day was it when Scrooge woke up?
    It was Christmas Day.

3. What did Scrooge ask the boy under his window to do, and why?
    He asked the boy to go to the Poulterer's and have them bring the prize turkey to his home. From there, he planned to have it sent to Bob Cratchit's house.

4. How did Scrooge act when he went outside?
    He was smiling and saying hello to people.

5. What did Scrooge do when he met the man who had asked for a donation the day before?
    He whispered an amount in the man's ear and asked the man to come and see him.

6. Whom did Scrooge visit? What was the reaction?
    He went to his nephew Fred's house. He asked if he could join them for dinner, and they agreed. He felt at home and had a wonderful time.

7. What happened at the office the next morning?
    Scrooge got there ahead of Bob Cratchit. When Bob got there, Scrooge said he would give him a raise. Scrooge also offered to help the family. He told Bob to buy another coal scuttle.

8. How did Scrooge spend the rest of his life?
    He became a good friend to many and a second father to Tiny Tim. He didn't see any more spirits.

MULTIPLE CHOICE STUDY/QUIZ QUESTIONS *A Christmas Carol*

<u>Stave 1 Marley's Ghost</u>

1. Who was Marley?
    A. Marley was Scrooge's older brother.
    B. Marley was Scrooge's business partner.
    C. Marley was Scrooge's father.
    D. Marley was Scrooge's boss.

2. What was Marley's condition at the beginning of the story?
    A. He had just discovered that he was bankrupt.
    B. He was in the hospital dying.
    C. He was recovering from pneumonia.
    D. He had been dead for seven years when the story opened.

3. What is the setting of the story?
    A. It takes place on Christmas Eve and Christmas Day in London. The year is not given.
    B. It takes place the week between Christmas and New Year's Day in Paris in 1654.
    C. It takes place during the week before Christmas in Boston in 1889.
    D. It takes place on Christmas Day in New York. The year is not given.

4. Who visited Scrooge at his warehouse, and what did he want? What was Scrooge's reply?
    A. Scrooge's younger brother came to ask for a job, because he had lost his. Scrooge refused. He said his brother was lazy and should take care of himself.
    B. Scrooge's nephew came to wish him a merry Christmas and invite him for Christmas dinner. He replied only "Good Afternoon" when the nephew invited Scrooge to dinner.
    C. Scrooge's former employer made a social visit. Scrooge bragged about his wealth. The man asked to borrow money and Scrooge refused.
    D. A beggar came asking for a place to spend the night. Scrooge said he could stay if he paid for the space. The beggar went away.

5. What did the other men who came to the warehouse want? What was Scrooge's reply to them?
    A. They wanted jobs. Scrooge said he would hire them and fire his clerk if they would agree to each work for half of the clerk's salary.
    B. They wanted Scrooge to give money to renovate the church. He told them he did not go to church and would not help to repair it.
    C. They asked for a donation for the poor and destitute. Scrooge replied that he did not make merry, and could not afford to help idle people make merry.
    D. Scrooge was the only businessman who kept his warehouse open on Christmas Day. They tried to persuade him to close, but he refused.

6. True or False: Scrooge told his clerk he could only have Christmas Day off if he took it without pay.
   A. True
   B. False

7. What happened when Scrooge was opening his door?
   A. The door opened by itself and Scrooge was pulled into the room.
   B. The key turned into a snake and then back into a key.
   C. The door knob became too hot to touch, and Scrooge had to kick the door in.
   D. The door knocker turned into Jacob Marley's face, then back to a door knocker.

8. True or False: Marley's ghost appeared. He told Scrooge he was doomed to travel the world forever and look at all of the kindness and happiness he had missed. He also said Scrooge was headed on the same path, but still had a chance to redeem himself.
   A. True
   B. False

9. The visitor told Scrooge about some other visitors who would be coming. Who were they? When would they come?
   A. Members of Scrooge's family would come for Christmas dinner.
   B. All of the people Scrooge had cheated in business were coming to the warehouse to get even with him. They would be there the next day.
   C. Three Spirits were to come, one each night for the next three nights.
   D. Two other versions of Scrooge would visit him in the morning. He would see how they acted and then decide which one he wanted to become.

10. What did Scrooge do after his visitor left?
    A. He hid under his bed.
    B. He lit all of the candles and stayed up all night praying.
    C. He went into the yard and buried his money. Then he went to the warehouse to stay.
    D. He looked out the window. Then he closed the window and went to sleep.

Christmas Carol Multiple Choice Questions

Stave Two The First of the Three Spirits

1. What did Scrooge notice about the church chimes when he woke up?
    A. The chimes went from six all the way to twelve, then stopped.
    B. They were silent, and they should have been ringing.
    C. They kept striking three over and over.
    D. They were playing Christmas carols instead of striking the hour.

2. Which of the following sentences does **not** describe the first Spirit?
    A. It was like a child and an old man at the same time.
    B. It had long white hair and a face without wrinkles.
    C. The Spirit wore a white tunic trimmed with summer flowers.
    D. There were jets of light coming from its hands.

3. True or False: The first Spirit was The Ghost of the First Christmas.
    A. True
    B. False

4. Scrooge asked the Spirit what business brought him there. What was the Spirit's answer?
    A. It said universal salvation brought it.
    B. It said it came to help the poor and destitute of the world.
    C. It said Scrooge's welfare and reclamation brought it.
    D. It said it had to do a good deed so it could rest in peace.

5. Which sentence describes the first scene Scrooge and the Spirit visited?
    A. It was the young boy who had been singing under Scrooge's window the night before.
    B. They saw Scrooge's parents soon after he had been born.
    C. They saw the city without any poverty.
    D. It was Scrooge's boyhood home and school. They saw Scrooge as a young boy, reading.

6. Who was Fan?
    A. Fan was Scrooge's mother.
    B. Fan was Scrooge's father.
    C. Fan was Scrooge's younger sister.
    D. Fan was Scrooge's brother.

7. True or False: Fezziwig was Scrooge's former master. He was hosting a Christmas party for his family and his employees.
    A. True
    B. False

8. What did Scrooge say to the Ghost about the scene?
    A. Scrooge said Fezziwig was crazy to spend his money that way.
    B. Scrooge said he never liked the way Fezziwig ran his business, so he did everything the opposite of what he had learned there.
    C. Scrooge said that Fezziwig had the power to make the others happy or unhappy. Scrooge said he wished he could talk to his clerk then.
    D. Scrooge said the things he saw had never really happened. He accused the Spirit of making them up.

9. True or False: Scrooge broke off his engagement to Belle because he wanted to keep all of his money for himself.
    A. True
    B. False

10. How did Scrooge try to get rid of the Ghost?
    A. He held a candle in front of its face and it disappeared.
    B. He took the holly sprig and threw it into the fireplace.
    C. He threw the Ghost's chain out the window.
    D. He took the extinguisher-cap and pressed it down on the Ghost's head.

Christmas Carol Multiple Choice Questions

<u>Stave Three The Second of the Three Spirits</u>
1. True or False: Scrooge was waiting in his bed when the hour stuck, but nothing happened. Then Scrooge noticed a blaze of light, and thought it was coming from the adjoining room. He opened the door and found the Sprit in there.
   A. True
   B. False

2. True or False: Scrooge and the second Spirit were in his room. The room was bare, dark, and cold.
   A. True
   B. False

3. Who was the second Spirit?
   A. It was the Spirit of the Christmas That Never Was.
   B. It was the Ghost of Cheerful Giving.
   C. It was the Spirit of the Holiday Here and Now.
   D. It was the Ghost of Christmas Present.

4. Which of the following sentences does **not** describe the second Spirit?
   A. It wore a green robe with a white fur border.
   B. It had bare feet.
   C. It had short, black, straight hair.
   D. It wore a holly wreath on its head.

5 Describe the first place they went.
   A. They went to the poorhouse.
   B. They went to the streets.
   C. They went to the town church.
   D. They went to the hospital.

6. What was the second place they visited?
   A. They visited the graveyard where Scrooge's parents were buried.
   B. They visited Scrooge's nephew.
   C. They visited Scrooge, sitting alone in his warehouse.
   D. They visited the home of Scrooge's clerk, Bob Cratchit.

7. Scrooge wanted to know if Tiny Tim would live or die. What was the Spirit's reply?
   A. The Ghost replied that if things did not change in the future, Tiny Tim would die.
   B. The Ghost said it did not know. The next Spirit would give the answer.
   C. The Ghost said there was no hope for Tiny Tim. He would die within a week.
   D. The Ghost said if Scrooge prayed for a miracle, Tiny Tim might live.

8. Bob Cratchit offered a toast to Scrooge, calling him "The Founder of the Feast." What was Mrs. Cratchit's response?
   A. She made the toast, but only because Bob asked her to.
   B. She was glad to toast him. She was happy Bob had a steady job.
   C. She refused because she said Scrooge didn't deserve to be toasted.
   D. She told Bob he would have to toast Scrooge somewhere else, not in her house.

9. What did Scrooge find at the other places he visited with the Spirit?
   A. He saw suffering and misery everywhere he went.
   B. He saw people toasting the Scrooge of that time for his generosity.
   C. He saw that the people at each location were happily celebrating Christmas.
   D. He saw an equal mix of happiness and sadness.

10. Someone Scrooge saw thought he was a "comical old fellow." He said he felt sorry for Scrooge, that he was the one who really suffered for his own ill whims. Others said they had no patience with him. Who were these people?
    A. The businessmen Scrooge knew said these things.
    B. The first two Spirits said these things.
    C. Scrooge's nephew and nieces said these things.
    D. Scrooge's sister and brother said these things.

11. True or False: Scrooge thought the harp music was annoying. He said listening to music put him in a bad mood.
    A. True
    B. False

12. What did Scrooge do while his nephew and the others were playing games?
    A. He sat in a corner and cried.
    B. He tried to ruin the games.
    C. He begged the Spirit to take him away.
    D. He joined in, even though they couldn't see or hear him.

13. True or False: Scrooge's nephew thought of something, and the rest had to find out what it was by asking questions that could be answered either "yes" or "no." Clues were that it was a live, disagreeable animal that lived in London. One of the nieces guessed that it was Scrooge.
    A. True
    B. False

14. How did Scrooge feel by the time he and the Spirit left his nephew's house?
    A. He was very depressed.
    B. He was a little bit excited.
    C. He was cheerful and light-hearted.
    D. He was angry at the Spirit for not letting him participate in the fun.

15. What happened to the way the Ghost and Scrooge looked as the night went on?
    A. Scrooge stayed the same but the Ghost got older.
    B. The Ghost got older but Scrooge got younger.
    C. They both got older.
    D. Scrooge became invisible and the Ghost became visible.

16. Who were the two children the Ghost had under its robe?
    A. They were boy twins of Jealousy and Hatred.
    B. The girl was Generosity and the boy was Compassion.
    C. They were both girls. One was Good and the other was Evil.
    D. The boy was Ignorance, and the girl was Want.

17. True or False: When Scrooge asked: "Have they no refuge or resource?" the Spirit replied with Scrooge's own early response: "Are there no prisons? Are there no workhouses?"
    A. True
    B. False

Christmas Carol Multiple Choice Questions

Stave 4 The Last of the Spirits

1. True or False: Scrooge feared this Ghost. His legs trembled, and he could hardly stand up.
    A. True
    B. False

2. What did the Ghost of Christmas Yet to Come look like?
    A. It was dressed in a purple robe. It was the same height as Scrooge, and did not speak.
    B. It was covered by a black garment. It was tall, and did not speak.
    C. It was shorter than Scrooge, had long white hair, a white robe, and talked all of the time.
    D. It was tall, wore a business suit like Scrooge's, and spoke in riddles.

3. Where did Scrooge and the Spirit go first?
    A. They went to the city.
    B. They went to the park.
    C. They went to the church.
    D. They went to Scrooge's warehouse.

4. The business men were talking about another businessman's (Old Scratch's) death. Which of the following was **not** talked about?
    A. One man asked when he died.
    B. Someone wondered what he had done with his money.
    C. They all wondered who would go to his funeral, since he had no friends.
    D. They all thought he had been murdered, and wondered who had done it.

5. True or False: Scrooge knew he would learn something for his own improvement. He treasured everything he heard and saw when he was with the third Spirit.
    A. True
    B. False

6. Which person was not with the old man in the shop?
    A. an undertaker's assistant
    B. a charwoman
    C. a gardener
    D. a laundress

7. True or False: Scrooge was furious at the people in the scene.
    A. True
    B. False

8. What did Scrooge think about when he saw the dead man?
    A. He wondered if the man knew that no one was sorry he died.
    B. He wondered if the man went to Heaven.
    C. He thought about his own death and vowed to make better preparations in the morning.
    D. He thought that avarice and hard dealing had caused an early death.

9. Scrooge asked the Spirit to show him someone who felt emotion at the man's death. Describe the person the Spirit showed him.
    A. It was the man's business partner. He was glad the man had died, because he would get the whole business.
    B. It was Scrooge just after Marley's death. Scrooge did not realize he was angry at Marley for leaving him.
    C. It was a man who owed money to the dead man. He and his wife were glad the lender was dead because they thought another creditor would have more mercy on them.
    D. It was the man's wife. She was glad she would not have to live with his meanness anymore.

10. Scrooge asked the Ghost to show him some tenderness connected with a death. What did the Ghost show him?
    A. The Ghost took him to the Cratchit home, where they were mourning the death of Tiny Tim.
    B. The Ghost took him to his mother's funeral, where he had mourned.
    C. The Ghost took him to a church where there was a funeral for Mr. Fezziwig. The entire family and all of his employees were there.
    D. The Ghost took him to see his own funeral in a time when he had become kind and generous. His family and many businessmen were there.

11. True or False: Scrooge's nephew was mean to Bob Cratchit when he heard about Tiny Tim's death. He told Bob he should be glad to have one less mouth to feed.
    A. True
    B. False

12. How did Scrooge discover who the dead man was?
    A. He heard the undertaker talking about who would pay the funeral bill.
    B. He saw the newspaper headline that said he had died.
    C. The Spirit told him.
    D. Scrooge read his name on the head stone at the graveyard.

13. What question did Scrooge ask the Ghost as they stood among the graves?
    A. He asked when the Spirit would be back again.
    B. He asked how he died.
    C. He asked if the shadow were of things that Will be or May be.
    D. He asked if the Spirits had visited any of the dead people in the graves.

14. What did Scrooge tell the Ghost he would do?
    A. He said he would celebrate all holidays except his birthday.
    B. He said he would pray to the three Spirits every day for guidance.
    C. He promised to honor Christmas and keep it all year.
    D. He said he would give away all of his money and live in poverty himself.

Christmas Carol Multiple Choice Questions

Stave 5 The End of It

1. True or False: Scrooge was sad and scared when he woke up.
    A. True
    B. False

2. What day was it when Scrooge woke up?
    A. It was New Year's Day.
    B. It was Christmas Day.
    C. It was three days after Christmas.
    D. It was Christmas Eve.

3. What was Scrooge planning to do with the prize turkey?
    A. He planned to have it sent to Bob Cratchit's house.
    B. He planned to cook it and have a party like the one he saw at Fezziwig's house.
    C. He planned to donate it to the church for the poor.
    D. He planned to take it to his nephew's house.

4. How did Scrooge act when he went outside?
    A. He hid his head and hoped people would not notice him.
    B. He was singing and dancing.
    C. He pretended to be like his old self, and went around saying "humbug."
    D. He was smiling and saying hello to people.

5. What did Scrooge do when he met the man who had asked for a donation the day before?
    A. He gave the man a bag full of coins.
    B. He pretended not to know him, because he was embarrassed.
    C. He whispered an amount in the man's ear and asked the man to come and see him.
    D. He apologized for his former behavior and gave the man a five pound note.

6. True or False: Scrooge went to his nephew Fred's house. He asked if he could join them for dinner, and they agreed. He felt at home and had a wonderful time.
    A. True
    B. False

7. Which of the following did **not** happen at the office the next morning?
    A. Scrooge said he would give Bob Cratchit a raise.
    B. Scrooge also offered to help the family.
    C. Scrooge offered a job to Peter Cratchit.
    D. Scrooge told Bob to buy another coal scuttle.

8. True or False: The Ghost of Jacob Marley visited Scrooge every year to make sure he kept his promises.
    A. True
    B. False

STUDENT ANSWER SHEET-MULTIPLE CHOICE/QUIZ QUESTIONS

Stave 1	Stave 2	Stave 3
Marley's Ghost	The First of the Three Spirits	The Second of the Three Spirits

Stave 1 — Marley's Ghost
1. _____
2.
3.
4.
5.
6.
7.
8.
9.
10.

Stave 2 — The First of the Three Spirits
1.
2.
3.
4.
5.
6.
7.
8.
9.
10.

Stave 3 — The Second of the Three Spirits
1.
2.
3.
4.
5.
6.
7.
8.
9.
10.
11.
12.
13.
14.
15.
16.
17.

Stave 4 — The Last of the Spirits
1.
2.
3.
4.
5.
6.
7.
8.
9.
10.
11.
12.
13.
14.

Stave 5 — The End of It
1.
2.
3.
4.
5.
6.
7.
8.

ANSWER KEY-MULTIPLE CHOICE/QUIZ QUESTIONS

	Stave 1 Marley's Ghost	Stave 2 The First of the Three Spirits	Stave 3 The Second of the Three Spirits
1.	B	A	A TRUE
2.	D	D	B FALSE
3.	A	B FALSE	D
4.	B	C	C
5.	C	D	B
6.	B FALSE	C	D
7.	D	A TRUE	A
8.	A TRUE	C	C
9.	C	B FALSE	C
10.	D	D	C
11.			B FALSE
12.			D
13.			A TRUE
14.			C
15.			A
16.			D
17.			A TRUE

ANSWER KEY –MULTIPLE CHOICE QUIZ QUESTIONS CONTINUED

<u>Stave 4</u>
<u>The Last of the Spirits</u>
1. A TRUE
2. B
3. A
4. D
5. A TRUE
6. C
7. B
8. D
9. C
10. A
11. B FALSE
12. D
13. C
14. C

<u>Stave 5</u>
<u>The End of It</u>
1. B FALSE
2. B
3. A
4. D
5. C
6. A TRUE
7. C
8. B FALSE

PREREADING VOCABULARY WORKSHEETS

Vocabulary Worksheets *A Christmas Carol*

Stave 1 Marley's Ghost
Part I: Using Prior Knowledge and Context Clues
Below are the sentences in which the vocabulary words appear in the text. Read the sentence. Use any clues you can find in the sentence combined with your prior knowledge, and write what you think the underlined words mean on the lines provided.

1. Oh, but he was a tightly-fisted hand at the grindstone, Scrooge! a squeezing, wrenching, grasping, scraping, clutching, *covetous* old sinner!

   _____

2. "What right have you to be dismal? What reason have you to be *morose*?"

   _____

3. "I am sorry, with all my heart, to find you so *resolute*."

   _____

4. He stopped at the outer door to bestow the feelings of the season on the clerk, who, cold as he was, was warmer than Scrooge; for he returned them *cordially*.

   _____

5. It certainly was; for they had been two *kindred* spirits.

   _____

6. At the *ominous* word "liberality," Scrooge frowned, and shook his head, and handed the credentials back.

   _____

7. "At this festive season of the year, Mr. Scrooge," said the gentleman, taking up a pen, "it is more than usually desirable that we should make some slight provision for the poor and *destitute*, who suffer greatly at the present time."

   _____

Vocabulary Worksheets *A Christmas Carol*

8. Scrooge could not feel it himself, but this was clearly the case; for though the Ghost sat perfectly motionless, its hair, and skirts, and tassels, were still *agitated* as by the hot vapour from an oven.

_____

9. "You are *fettered*," said Scrooge, trembling. "Tell me why." "I wear the chain I forged in life," replied the Ghost.

_____

10. "Oh, captive, bound, and double-ironed," cried the phantom, "not to know, that ages of incessant labour by immortal creatures, for this earth must pass into eternity before the good of which it is *susceptible* is all developed."

_____

Part II: Determining the Meaning Match the vocabulary words to their dictionary definitions.

_____ 1. covetous   A. poor; penniless
_____ 2. morose   B. determined
_____ 3. resolute   C. shackled; chained
_____ 4. cordially   D. avaricious; eagerly desirous of; greedy
_____ 5. kindred   E. threatening
_____ 6. ominous   F. stirred up; disturbed
_____ 7. destitute   G. impressionable; easily influenced
_____ 8. agitated   H. related; belonging to the same family
_____ 9. fettered   I. ill-humored; sullen
_____ 10. susceptible   J. graciously; in a friendly way

Vocabulary Worksheets *A Christmas Carol*

Stave 2 The First of the Three Spirits
Part I: Using Prior Knowledge and Context Clues
Below are the sentences in which the vocabulary words appear in the text. Read the sentence. Use any clues you can find in the sentence combined with your prior knowledge, and write what you think the underlined words mean on the lines provided.

1. The curtains of his bed were drawn aside; and Scrooge, starting up into a half-*recumbent* attitude, found himself face to face with the unearthly visitor who drew them: as close to it as I am now to you, and I am standing in the spirit at your elbow.

   _____

2. It would have been in vain for Scrooge to plead that the weather and the hour were not adapted to *pedestrian* purposes; that bed was warm, and the thermometer a long way below freezing; that he was clad but lightly in his slippers, dressing gown, and nightcap; and that he had a cold upon him at the time.

   _____

3. He rose: but finding that the Spirit made towards the window, clasped its robe in *supplication*. "I am a mortal," Scrooge remonstrated, "and liable to fall."

   _____

4. He rose: but finding that the Spirit made towards the window, clasped its robe in supplication. "I am a mortal," Scrooge *remonstrated*, "and liable to fall."

   _____

5. It opened before them, and disclosed a long, bare, *melancholy* room, made barer still by lines of plain deal forms and desks.

   _____

6. A terrible voice in the hall cried, "Bring down Master Scrooge's box, there!" and in the hall appeared the schoolmaster himself, who glared on Master Scrooge with a ferocious *condescension,* and threw him into a dreadful state of mind by shaking hands with him.

   _____

7. He rubbed his hands; adjusted his *capacious* waistcoat; laughed all over himself, from his shoes to his organ of benevolence; and called out in a comfortable, oily, rich, fat, jovial voice: "Yo ho, there! Ebenezer! Dick!"

_____

8. He rubbed his hands; adjusted his capacious waistcoat; laughed all over himself, from his shoes to his organ of *benevolence*; and called out in a comfortable, oily, rich, fat, jovial voice: "Yo ho, there! Ebenezer! Dick!"

_____

9. "All your other hopes have merged into the hope of being beyond the chance of its *sordid* reproach. . . . "

_____

10. In the struggle, if that can be called a struggle in which the Ghost with no visible resistance on its own part was undisturbed by any effort of its *adversary*, Scrooge observed that its light was burning high and bright . . .

_____

Part II: Determining the Meaning Match the vocabulary words to their dictionary definitions.

___ 1.	recumbent	A.	reclining; lying down
___ 2.	pedestrian	B.	filthy; vile
___ 3.	supplication	C.	sadness; depression ; gloom
___ 4.	remonstrated	D.	asking for humbly or earnestly; praying
___ 5.	melancholy	E.	opponent; enemy
___ 6.	condescension	F.	going on foot; walking
___ 7.	capacious	G.	generosity; kindness
___ 8.	benevolence	H.	being courteous with a superior air
___ 9.	sordid	I.	spacious; large
___ 10.	adversary	J.	protested

Vocabulary Worksheets *A Christmas Carol*

Stave 3 The Second of the Three Spirits
Part I: Using Prior Knowledge and Context Clues
Below are the sentences in which the vocabulary words appear in the text. Read the sentence. Use any clues you can find in the sentence combined with your prior knowledge, and write what you think the underlined words mean on the lines provided.

1. Awaking in the middle of a *prodigiously* tough snore, and sitting up in the bed to get his thoughts together, Scrooge had no occasion to be told that the bell was again upon the stroke of One.

   _____

2. . . . and was sometimes apprehensive that he might be at that very moment an interesting case of spontaneous combustion, without having the *consolation* of knowing it.

   _____

3. This garment hung so loosely on the figure, that its capacious breast was bare, as if *disdaining* to be warded or concealed by any artifice.

   _____

4. For the people who were shovelling away on the housetops were jovial and full of glee. . . and now and then exchanging a *facetious* snowball--better-natured missile far than many a wordy jest. . . .

   _____

5. "Why, bless your heart alive, my dear, how late you are!" said Mrs. Crachit, kissing her a dozen times, and taking off her shawl and bonnet for her, with *officious* zeal.

   _____

6. . . . Master Peter, and the two *ubiquitous* young Crachits went to fetch the goose, with which they soon returned in high procession.

   _____

7. Suppose somebody should have got over the wall of the back-yard, and stolen it, while they were merry with the goose; a supposition at which the two young Crachits became *livid*!

_____

8. "It should be Christmas Day, I am sure," said she, "on which one drinks the health of such an *odious*, stingy, hard, unfeeling man as Mr. Scrooge."

_____

9. But when at last he caught her; when, in spite of all her silken rustlings, and her rapid flutterings past him, he got her into a corner whence there was no escape; then his conduct was the most *execrable*.

_____

10. In almshouse, hospital, and jail, in misery's every refuge, where vain man in his little brief authority had not made fast the door, and barred the Spirit out, he left his blessing, and taught Scrooge his *precepts*.

_____

Part II: Determining the Meaning Match the vocabulary words to their dictionary definitions.

____ 1.	prodigiously	A.	very bad; offensive
____ 2.	consolation	B.	comfort; compassion
____ 3.	disdaining	C.	meddlesome; self-important
____ 4.	facetious	D.	humorous; merry
____ 5.	officious	E.	hateful
____ 6.	ubiquitous	F.	treating with scorn or contempt
____ 7.	livid	G.	practical rules guiding conduct
____ 8.	odious	H.	being everywhere
____ 9.	execrable	I.	enormously; hugely
____ 10.	precepts	J.	angry; furious

Vocabulary Worksheets *A Christmas Carol*

Stave 4 The Last of the Spirits
Part I: Using Prior Knowledge and Context Clues
Below are the sentences in which the vocabulary words appear in the text. Read the sentence. Use any clues you can find in the sentence combined with your prior knowledge, and write what you think the underlined words mean on the lines provided.

1. They scarcely seemed to enter the city; for the city rather seemed to spring up about them, and *encompass* them of its own act.

   _____

2. But nothing doubting that to whomsoever they applied they had some *latent* moral for his own improvement, he resolved to treasure up every word he heard. . . .

   _____

3. They left the busy scene, and went into an *obscure* part of the town, where Scrooge had never penetrated before although he recognised its situation, and its bad repute.

   _____

4. Far in this den of *infamous* resort, there was a low-browed, beetling shop, below a pent-house roof, where iron, old rags, bottles, bones, and greasy offal, were brought.

   _____

5. "I ain't so fond of his company that I'd *loiter* about him for such things, if he did."

   _____

6. As they sat grouped about their spoil, in the scanty light afforded by the old man's lamp, he viewed them with a *detestation* and disgust, which could hardly have been greater, though they had been obscene demons, marketing the corpse itself.

   _____

7. "If he *relents*," she said, amazed, "there is! Nothing is past hope, if such a miracle has happened."

_____

8. Spirit of Tiny Tim, thy childish *essence* was from God!

_____

9. The *inexorable* finger underwent no change.

_____

10. "Your nature *intercedes* for me, and pities me."

_____

Part II: Determining the Meaning   Match the vocabulary words to their dictionary definitions.

_____ 1. encompass   A. softens in attitude or temper
_____ 2. latent   B. dark; vague; unclear
_____ 3. obscure   C. relentless; unyielding
_____ 4. infamous   D. dormant; hidden
_____ 5. loiter   E. spirit
_____ 6. detestation   F. hang around; linger
_____ 7. relents   G. pleads on another's behalf
_____ 8. essence   H. intense dislike; aversion
_____ 9. inexorable   I. to surround
_____ 10. intercedes   J. notoriously bad

Vocabulary Worksheets *A Christmas Carol*

Stave 5 The End of It
Part I: Using Prior Knowledge and Context Clues
Below are the sentences in which the vocabulary words appear in the text. Read the sentence. Use any clues you can find in the sentence combined with your prior knowledge, and write what you think the underlined words mean on the lines provided.

1. They are here; I am here; the shadows of the things that would have been, may be *dispelled*.

2. His hands were busy with his garments all this time; turning them inside out, putting them on upside down, tearing them, mislaying them, making them parties to every kind of *extravagance*.

3. Really, for a man who had been out of practice for so many years, it was a splendid laugh, a most *illustrious* laugh.

4. The chuckle with which he said this, and the chuckle with which he paid for the Turkey, and the chuckle with which he paid for the cab, and the chuckle with which he *recompensed* the boy, were only to be exceeded by the chuckle with which he sat down breathless in his chair again, and chuckled till he cried.

5. And Scrooge said often afterwards, that all of the *blithe* sounds he had ever heard, those were the blithest in his ears.

6. He had not gone far, when coming on towards him he beheld the *portly* gentleman, who had walked into his counting-house the day before and said, "Scrooge and Marley's, I believe?"

7. So did everyone when they came. Wonderful party, wonderful games, wonderful *unanimity*, won-der-ful happiness!

_____

8. "Hallo!" growled Scrooge, in his accustomed voice as near as he could *feign* it.

_____

9. Some people laughed to see the *alteration* in him, but he let them laugh, and little heeded them; for he was wise enough to know that nothing ever happened on this globe, for good, at which some people did not have their fill of laughter at the outset. . . .

_____

10. He had no further intercourse with Spirits, but lived upon the Total *Abstinence* Principle, ever afterwards, and it was always said of him, that he knew how to keep Christmas well, if any man alive possessed the knowledge.

_____

Part II: Determining the Meaning Match the vocabulary words to their dictionary definitions.

_____ 1. dispelled   A. glorious; brilliant
_____ 2. extravagance   B. stout; fat
_____ 3. illustrious   C. change
_____ 4. recompensed   D. pretend
_____ 5. blithe   E. repaid
_____ 6. portly   F. complete agreement
_____ 7. unanimity   G. avoidance
_____ 8. feign   H. extremely abundant; excessive
_____ 9. alteration   I. joyous; happy
_____ 10. abstinence   J. scattered; caused to vanish

STUDENT ANSWER SHEET-MULTIPLE CHOICE/QUIZ QUESTIONS *A Christmas Carol*

Stave 1
Marley's Ghost

1. _____
2. _____
3. _____
4. _____
5. _____
6. _____
7. _____
8. _____
9. _____
10. _____

Stave 2
The First of the Three Spirits

1. _____
2. _____
3. _____
4. _____
5. _____
6. _____
7. _____
8. _____
9. _____
10. _____

Stave 3
The Second of the Three Spirits

1. _____
2. _____
3. _____
4. _____
5. _____
6. _____
7. _____
8. _____
9. _____
10. _____

Stave 4
The Last of the Spirits

1. _____
2. _____
3. _____
4. _____
5. _____
6. _____
7. _____
8. _____
9. _____
10. _____

Stave 5
The End of It

1. _____
2. _____
3. _____
4. _____
5. _____
6. _____
7. _____
8. _____
9. _____
10. _____

ANSWER KEY-PREREADING VOCABULARY WORKSHEETS *A Christmas Carol*

Stave 1
Marley's Ghost

1. D
2. I
3. B
4. J
5. H
6. E
7. A
8. F
9. C
10. G

Stave 2
The First of the Three Spirits

1. A
2. F
3. D
4. J
5. C
6. H
7. I
8. G
9. B
10. E

Stave 3
The Second of the Three Spirits

1. I
2. B
3. F
4. D
5. C
6. H
7. J
8. E
9. A
10. G

Stave 4
The Last of the Spirits

1. I
2. D
3. B
4. J
5. F
6. H
7. A
8. E
9. C
10. G

Stave 5
The End of It

1. J
2. H
3. A
4. E
5. I
6. B
7. F
8. D
9. C
10. G

EXTRA VOCABULARY WORDS

Note to the Teacher: The following words are not tested. However, since some of them may be difficult for the students, and understanding them is necessary to the story, the context from the story and the definition are included in this supplement.

<u>Stave 1 Marley's Ghost</u>

1. <u>*stave*</u>

   a set of verses

2. You will therefore permit me to repeat, <u>*emphatically*</u>, that Marley was as dead as a door-nail.

   very definitely

3. The cold within him froze his old features, tipped his pointed nose, shrivelled his cheek, stiffened his <u>gait,</u> made his eyes red, his thin lips blue; and spoke out shrewdly in his grating voice.

   step; stride; pace

4. A frosty <u>*rime*</u> was on his head, and on his eyebrows, and his wiry chin.

   A coating of ice formed when extremely cold water droplets freeze instantly on a cold surface.

5. . . . and candles were flaring in the windows of the neighbouring offices, like <u>*ruddy*</u> smears upon the <u>*palpable*</u> brown air.

   red-colored; rosy
   able to be handled, touched, or felt

6. The door of Scrooge's counting house was open that he might keep his eye upon his clerk, who in a <u>*dismal*</u> little cell beyond, a sort of tank, was copying letters.

   dreary; depressing

7. "But I am sure I have always thought of Christmas time, when it has come round--apart from the *veneration* due to its sacred name and origin, if anything belonging to it can be apart from that--as a good time. . . . "

   reverence; devotion; honor

8. "But I have made the trial in *homage* to Christmas, and I'll keep my Christmas humour to the last."

   tribute; honor

9. He stopped outside the door to *bestow* the greetings of the season on the clerk, who, cold as he was, was warmer than Scrooge; for he returned them cordially.

   give; offer

10. "If they would rather die," said Scrooge, "they had better do it, and decrease the *surplus* population."

    excess; extra

11. The water plug being left in solitude, its overflowings sullenly *congealed*, and turned to *misanthropic* ice.

    hardened; frozen
    hatred or mistrust of mankind

12. Scrooge seized the ruler with such energy of action, that the singer fled in terror, leaving the keyhole to the fog and even more *congenial* frost.

    sociable; friendly

13. With an ill-will Scrooge dismounted from his stool, and *tacitly* admitted the fact to the expectant clerk in the Tank, who instantly snuffed his candle out, and put on his hat.

    silently

14. Scrooge took his *melancholy* dinner in his usual melancholy tavern; and having read all the newspapers, *beguiled* the rest of the evening with his banker's-book, went home to bed.

    sad; depressed
    charmed; tricked

15. But he put his hand upon the key he had *relinquished*, turned it sturdily, walked in, and lighted his candle.

    given up, let go

16. To sit, staring at those fixed, glazed eyes, in silence for a moment, would play, Scrooge felt, the very *deuce* with him.

    an expression of anger; to the devil

17. There was something very awful, too, in the spectre's being provided with an *infernal* atmosphere of its own.

    of or relating to the lower world of the dead

18. Incessant torture of *remorse*.

    sorrow; misery

19. ". . It is a ponderous chain."

    heavy; massive; weighty

20. "A chance and hope of my *procuring*, Ebenezer."

    bringing about

21. Scrooge's *countenance* fell almost as low as the Ghost's had done.

    face; expression

22. "Without their visits," said the Ghost, "you cannot hope to *shun* the path I tread."

    avoid

23. Not so much in obedience, as in surprise and fear, for on the raising of the hand, he became sensible of confused noises in the air; incoherent sounds of *lamentation* and regret; wailings inexpressibly sorrowful and self-accusatory.

moaning; wailing

Stave 2 The First of the Three Spirits

1. When Scrooge awoke, it was so dark, that looking out of bed, he could scarcely distinguish the *transparent* window from the *opaque* walls of his chamber.

easily seen through
dark; not reflecting light

2. It was a strange figure--like a child; yet not so like a child as like an old man, viewed through some supernatural *medium*, which gave him the appearance of having *receded* from the view, and being diminished to a child's proportions.

means of expression
move back or away from

3. "I was *bred* in this place. I was a boy here."

brought up

4. "Remember it!" cried Scrooge with *fervour*--"I could walk it blindfold."

warm, intense emotion

5. The *jocund* travellers came on; and as they came, Scrooge knew and named them every one.

lighthearted

6. Nor was it more *retentive of* its ancient state, within; for entering the dreary hall, and glancing through the open doors of many rooms, they found them poorly furnished, cold, and vast.

keeping in a particular condition

7. Not a *latent* echo in the house, not a squeak and scuffle from the mice behind the panelling, not a drip from the half-thawed water-spout in the dull yard behind, not a sigh among the leafless boughs of one *despondent* poplar, not the idle swinging of an empty store-house door. . . .

   present but not evident
   sad; melancholy; depressed

8. Then she began to drag him, in her childish eagerness, towards the door, and he, nothing *loth* to go, accompanied her.

   unwilling; reluctant

9. "Always a delicate creature, whom a breath might have *withered*," said the Ghost.

   dried up or shriveled

10. But *scorning* rest upon his reappearance, he instantly began again, though there were no dancers yet, as if the other fiddler had been carried home, exhausted. . . . .

    showing contempt

11. "It isn't that," said Scrooge, "heated by the remark, and speaking unconsciously like his *former*, not his *latter*, self."

    earlier; first of two things
    second of two things

12. "There is nothing on which it is so hard as poverty; and there is nothing it professes to condemn with such *severity* as the pursuit of wealth!"

    harshness

13. But the relentless Ghost *pinioned* him in both his arms, and forced him to observe what happened next.

    held down; restrained

14. The noise in this room was perfectly *tumultuous*, for there were more children there. . . .

    noisy; uproarious

15. He gave the cap a parting squeeze, in which his had relaxed; and had barely time to *reel* to bed, before he sank into a heavy sleep.

   stagger

Stave 3 The Second of the Three Spirits

1. ... and was sometimes apprehensive that he might be at that very moment an interesting case of *spontaneous combustion*, without having the consolation of knowing it.

   an unplanned or sudden burning

2. The moment Scrooge's hand was on the lock, a strange voice called him by his name, and *bade* him enter.

   invited

3. ... and such a mighty blaze went roaring up the chimney, as that dull *petrification* of a hearth had never known in Scrooge's time. ...

   fossilized; wood that has been converted into a stony replica

4. This garment hung so loosely on the figure, that its capacious breast was bare, as if disdaining to be *warded* or concealed by any *artifice*.

   protected
   scheme; strategy

5. ... furrows that crossed and re-crossed each other hundreds of times where the great streets branched off, and made *intricate* channels, hard to trace, in the thick yellow mud and icy water.

   complex; puzzling

6. ... there were bunches of grapes, made in shopkeepers' *benevolence* to dangle from *conspicuous* hooks, that people's mouths might water *gratis* as they passed. ...

   kindness; generosity
   noticeable
   free

7. ... the candied fruits so caked and spotted with molten sugar as to make the coldest on-lookers feel faint and subsequently *bilious*.

   having an upset stomach

8. Scrooge hung his head to hear his own words quoted by the Spirit, and was overcome with *penitence* and grief.

   sorrow; contrition

9. Scrooge bent before the Ghost's *rebuke* and trembling *cast* his eyes upon the ground.

   scolding; reprimand
   to look down

10. Down in the west the setting sun had left a streak of fiery red, which glared upon the *desolation* for an instant, like a *sullen* eye, and frowning lower, lower, lower yet, was lost in the thick gloom of darkest night.

    bleakness; gloom
    irritable; moody

11. The Spirit did not *tarry* here, but bade Scrooge hold his robe. . . .

    delay; stop

12. When Scrooge's nephew laughed in this way; holding his sides, rolling his head, and twisting his face into the most *extravagant contortions*. . . .

    excessive; lavish
    twisting or bending out of shape

13. The way he went after that plump sister in the lace tucker, was an outrage on the *credulity* of human nature.

    believability

14. ... he would have made a *feint* of endeavouring to seize you...

    bluff; trick

15. . . . and wasn't led by anybody, and didn't live in a *menagerie* . . . .

   a diverse group

Stave 4 The Last of the Spirits
1. The night is *waning* fast, and it is precious time to me, I know.

   ending

2. "What has he done with his money?" asked a red-faced gentleman with a *pendulous excrescence* on the end of his nose, that shook like the gills of a turkey-cock.

   hanging loosely
   a wart or growth

3. But the *gallantry* of her friends would not allow of this; and the man in faded black, mounting the breach first, produced his *plunder*.

   courteous attention
   stolen property

4. "If *calico* an't good enough for such a purpose, it isn't good enough for anything."

   a rough cloth with a bright print

5. He *recoiled* in terror, for the scene had changed, and now he almost touched a bed. . . .

   to shrink or fall back

6. *Avarice*, hard dealing, griping cares?

   greed

Stave 5 The End of It
1. "The Spirits of all Three shall *strive* within me."

   try

2. "I didn't know what to do!" cried Scrooge, laughing and crying in the same breath; and making a perfect *Laocoön* of himself with his stockings.

   The Laocoön is an 8 foot high marble statue which was made around the first or second century BC. It shows Laocoön, a Trojan priest of Apollo, and his two sons, being attacked and killed by serpents. His death was a punishment from Athena for throwing a spear at the Trojan Horse. The serpents on the statue wind and twist around Laocoön and his sons. The Laocoön is in the Vatican Museum in Rome, Italy.

3. "Come back with the man, and I'll give you a *shilling*."

   a British coin worth one twentieth of a pound

4. "Come back with him in less than five minutes, and I'll give you a half-a-*crown*."

   a formerly used British coin worth five shillings

5. "Not a *farthing* less."

   a formerly used British coin worth one fourth of a penny

6. Some people laughed to see the alteration in him, but he let them laugh, and little *heeded* them. . . .

   thought about; paid attention to

7. He had no further *intercourse* with Spirits, but lived upon the Total Abstinence Principle, ever afterwards. . . .

   communication; association

64

DAILY LESSONS

LESSON ONE

Student Objectives
    1. To preview the *A Christmas Carol* unit
    2. To receive books and other related materials
    3. To relate prior knowledge to the new material
    4. To become acquainted with Project Tiny Tim

Activity #1

    Prior to class, decorate the bulletin board. Divide it in half. On one half, put up pictures of wealthy people enjoying the holidays (perhaps skiing, fancy parties, lots of jewelry and wrapped packages). On the other half, show poor people at holiday time (perhaps homeless, children with only one small toy, children with no coats, people standing in a food line at a soup kitchen.) Direct attention to the bulletin board. Ask students to describe what they see. Encourage students to discuss the differences in the ways people spend the holidays, and what people who are more fortunate can do to help the less fortunate. Tell them the novel is about a wealthy man, Ebenezer Scrooge, who does not like to share his wealth at the beginning of the story.

Activity #2

    Distribute the materials students will use in this unit. Explain in detail how students are to use these materials.

    Study Guides Students should preview the study guide questions before each reading assignment to get a feeling for what events and ideas are important in that section. After reading the section, students will (as a class or individually) answer the questions to review the important events and ideas from that section of the book. Students should keep the study guides as study materials for the unit test.

    Reading Assignment Sheet You need to fill in the reading assignment sheet to let students know when their reading has to be completed. You can either write the assignment sheet on a side blackboard or bulletin board and leave it there for students to see each day, or you can duplicate copies for each student to have. In either case, you should advise students to become very familiar with the reading assignments so they know what is expected of them.

    Extra Activities Center The Unit Resources portion of this unit contains suggestions for a library of related books and articles in your classroom as well as crossword and word search puzzles. Make an extra activities center in your room where you will keep these materials for students to use. (Bring the books and articles in from the library and keep several copies of the puzzles on hand.) Explain to students that these materials are available for students to use when they finish reading assignments or other class work early.

Books Each school has its own rules and regulations regarding student use of school books. Advise students of the procedures that are normal for your school.

Notebook or Unit Folder You may want the students to keep all of their worksheets, notes, and other papers for the unit together in a binder or notebook. During the first class meeting, tell them how you want them to arrange the folder. Make divider pages for vocabulary worksheets, prereading study guide questions, review activities, notes, and tests. You may want to give a grade for accuracy in keeping the folder.

Activity #3

Do a group KWL sheet with the students (form included.) Some students will know things about Charles Dickens and/or his books and will have information to share. Put this information in the K column (What I Know.) Ask students what they want to find out from reading the book and record this in the Q (What I Want to Find Out.) Keep the sheet and refer back to it after reading the book. Complete the L column (What I Learned) at that time.

Activity #4

Introduce Project Tiny Tim. Ask for input and ideas from the students.

KWL *A Christmas Carol*

Directions: Before reading, think about what you already know about Charles Dickens and/or *A Christmas Carol* Write the information in the K column. Think about what you would like to find out from reading the book. Write your questions in the W column. After you have read the book, use the L column to write the answers to your questions from the W column, and anything else you remember from the book.

K **What I Know**	**W** **What I Want** **to Find Out**	**L** **What I Learned**

PROJECT TINY TIM

Objectives:
      Project Tiny Tim is a total class project for use in conjunction with the novel *A Christmas Carol*. Since one of the main themes in the book deals with extending goodwill and kindness to others, especially the less fortunate, it seems the perfect occasion to make students aware of people in their own cities or towns who are in need. This project is intended to help students see the problem and have some part, however small, in really helping to do something about the problem.

THE PROJECT
      This project is separate from the rest of the *A Christmas Carol* unit so you can either use it while you are doing the A Christmas Carol unit or as a separate mini-unit after you have completed the unit test for the book. Also, having it as a separate project enables you to eliminate it if you want to or need to for some reason, without disrupting the normal flow of the unit.

Assignment 1 Your local TV station should have some videotaped reports about the sick or needy in your area (children with incurable diseases, elderly in nursing homes, etc.) Find several videotaped reports and show them to your students. Use the videotapes as a springboard for a discussion of the plight of the sick and/or needy.

Assignment 2 Use the local telephone book or a source book of resources from the city/town to find all of the agencies that help the poor and needy. Also get a list of any hospitals, nursing homes, and retirement communities in the area.

Assignment 3 Have the students call or write to the various agencies and find out what kind of volunteer help they use. Then have the students report their findings to the class.

Assignment 4 Have the students decide as a group which agency/ facility they would like to work with, and what they would like to do. Some suggestions are: making holiday cards, going to the place to read or sing, making a videotape of holiday songs or a play, holding a canned food or new toy drive, making holiday decorations and decorating the facility, arranging for students to make a series of visits. The planning of these activities should be done in class. Breaking down your class into groups to handle different activities would be a good idea if you are going to try to do more than one activity.
      A certain amount of class time will have to be spent on these plans. It should be a valuable experience for the students because they will be facing real problems and having to make real decisions concerning real solutions. Organization and scheduling skills will be used; in some cases, letter-writing and other communication skills will be applied. Again, the skills used will depend on how involved you make the project and what kinds of projects your students are interested in doing.

Assignment 5 Help students draft a letter outlining their plan. Send it to the agency or facility.

Assignment 6 Have students carry out the plans they have made. The types of activities they have planned will determine the amount of class time which will be spent on this project. If most of the work is being done outside of the classroom, be sure to get daily updates from each of your groups and occasionally have a day devoted to Project Tiny Tim work.

Assignment 7 When your Project Tiny Tim activities are complete, take a day to evaluate the success of the project. Discuss the good points and how things could have been done better. You may want to have a writing assignment in which each student evaluates his/her own experiences from the project.

LESSON TWO

Student Objectives
    1. To become familiar with the vocabulary for Stave 1
    2. To preview the study questions for Stave 1
    3. To read Stave 1

Activity #1
    Work through the prereading vocabulary worksheet for Stave 1 with the students. Tell them they will have a sheet like it to complete before reading each section of the book.

Activity #2
    Show students how to preview the study questions for Stave 1. Encourage them to predict what they think answers might be, to write down their predictions, and to compare them with their answers after reading the chapter.

Activity #3
    You may want to read the first few pages of Stave 1 aloud to the students to set the mood for the novel. Then invite willing students to read aloud to the rest of the class. Students with some acting ability may enjoy the challenge of reading aloud using a British accent. If students finish the reading early, allow them to begin answering the study questions.

LESSON THREE

<u>Student Objectives</u>

    1. To review the main themes and ideas in Stave 1
    2. To become familiar with the Non-fiction Writing Assignment
    3. To practice writing to inform
    4. To learn to do library research

Activity #1

    Give the students time to answer the study guide questions, and then discuss the answers in detail. Write the answers on the board or overhead projector so students can have the correct answers for study purposes. Encourage students to take notes.

    Note: It is a good practice in public speaking and leadership skills for individuals students to take charge of leading the discussion of the study questions. A different student could go to the front of the class and lead the discussion each day that the study questions are discussed during this unit. The teacher should guide the discussion and fill in any gaps the students leave.

Activity #2

    Distribute copies of the Nonfiction Assignment sheet and go over it in detail with the students. Explain to students that they each are to read at least one nonfiction piece, write a report about it, and fill in the Nonfiction Assignment Sheet. The report will count as one of the three unit writing assignments, Writing to Inform. They will also present their information to the class in the form of an oral report during Lesson 17. The nonfiction piece could be a book, a magazine article, or information from an encyclopedia or the Internet. Also consider letting students watch an educational television show or video, such as a documentary. Give them the due date for the assignment (Lesson 10 for the writing assignment, Lesson 17 for the Nonfiction Assignment Sheet and Oral Report.)

    Encourage students to research topics that are related to the novel. Some suggestions are: social conditions in England in the 19th century, the life of Charles Dickens, holiday celebrations from around the world, the class system in England, children's games and toys in the 19th century, child labor, British currency, treatment of the poor in the 19th century and the present time. You may want to make this a partner or small group project. Make sure students understand that they will all receive the same grade if they work in a group.

Activity #3

    Distribute copies of Writing Assignment #1. Go over the assignment in detail with the students. Tell them they will have the remainder of the class period to begin working on the assignment. Give the due date for the completed assignment. It should be a few days before the writing conferences, which are scheduled for Lesson 10.

Activity #4

Distribute copies of the Writing Evaluation Form (included with this Unit Plan.) Explain to students that during Lesson 10 you will be holding individual writing conferences about this writing assignment. Make sure students are familiar with the criteria on the Writing Evaluation Form.

Follow Up After you have graded the assignments, have a writing conference with each student. This Unit Plan schedules one in Lesson 10. After the writing conference, allow students to revise their papers using your suggestions to complete the revisions. Grade the revisions on an A-C-E scale: A = all revisions well done; C = some revisions made; E = few or no revisions made. This will speed your grading time and still give some credit for the students' efforts.

WRITING ASSIGNMENT #1 *A Christmas Carol*
Writing to Inform

PROMPT
You are reading about Ebenezer Scrooge, who learned something about the meaning of Christmas. The setting for the story is London. Although the exact date is not given, the story was originally published in 1843. The descriptions are those of typical 19th century life.

PREWRITING
Choose a topic or topics that interest you. Go to the library and find as many sources as you can on the topic. Look for encyclopedias, books, magazine articles, videos, and Internet sources. You may want to interview an expert on the topic of your choice.

Think of questions you have about your topic. Write each one on a separate index card. Then read to find the answers, and write them on the cards. Also take notes on interesting and important facts, even if you did not have questions about them. Put each fact on a separate card. Make sure to cite your references. That means to write down the source and the page number for each one.

Arrange your note card in the order you want to use for your paper.

DRAFTING
Introduce your topic in the first paragraph. Tell why you chose it, and give a preview of what the rest of the paper will be about. Then write several paragraphs about the topic. Each paragraph should have a main idea and supporting details. Your last paragraph should summarize the information in the report.

PEER CONFERENCE/REVISING
When you finish the rough draft, ask another student to look at it. You may want to give the student your note cards so he/she can double check for you and see that you have included all of the information. After reading, he or she should tell you what he/she liked best about your report, which parts were difficult to understand or needed more information, and ways in which your work could be improved. Reread your report considering your critic's comments and make the corrections you think are necessary.

PROOFREADING/EDITING
Do a final proofreading of your report, double-checking your grammar, spelling, organization, and the clarity of your ideas.

FINAL DRAFT
Follow your teacher's directions for making a final copy of your report.

NONFICTION ASSIGNMENT SHEET *A Christmas Carol*
(To be completed after reading the required nonfiction article)

Name _____ Date _____ Class _____

Title of Nonfiction Read _____

Written By _____ Publication Date _____

I. Factual Summary: Write a short summary of the piece you read.

II. Vocabulary:
  1. With which vocabulary words in the piece did you encounter some degree of difficulty?

  2. How did you resolve your lack of understanding with these words?

III. Interpretation: What was the main point the author wanted you to get from reading his/her work?

IV. Criticism:
  1. With which points of the piece did you agree or find easy to accept? Why?

  2. With which points of the piece did you disagree or find difficult to believe? Why?

V. Personal Response: What do you think about this piece? OR How does this piece influence your ideas?

WRITING EVALUATION FORM *A Christmas Carol*

Name _____ Date _____ Class _____

Circle One For Each Item:

Introduction	excellent	good	fair	poor
Body Paragraphs	excellent	good	fair	poor
Summary	excellent	good	fair	poor
Grammar	excellent	good	fair	poor (errors noted)
Spelling	excellent	good	fair	poor (errors noted)
Punctuation	excellent	good	fair	poor (errors noted)
Legibility	excellent	good	fair	poor (errors noted)

Strengths:

Weaknesses:

Comments/Suggestions:

LESSON FOUR

Objectives
    1. To preview the study questions for Stave 2
    2. To familiarize students with the vocabulary in Stave 2
    3. To read Stave 2 aloud for evaluation purposes
    4. To practice correct intonation and expression in oral reading

Activity #1

    Give students about fifteen minutes to preview the study questions for Stave 2 and do the related vocabulary work. Students can work individually or in groups.

Activity #2

    Have students read Stave 2 of *A Christmas Carol* out loud in class. You probably know the best way to get readers with your class; pick students at random, ask for volunteers, or use whatever method works best for your group. Since much of the book is written in dialog, you may want to have different students read the parts of the characters, and also the narrator. If you have not yet completed an oral reading evaluation for your students for this marking period, this would be a good opportunity to do so. A form is included with this unit for your convenience.

LESSON FIVE

Objectives
1. To review the main ideas and themes in Stave 2
2. To construct a story map

Activity #1
Allow students to work in small groups and go over the answers to the study questions. They should refer to the text if there are disagreements about any of the answers. When all groups have finished checking the answers, briefly check the answers with the whole class.

Activity #2
Introduce the story map handout (included.) You may want to make an overhead transparency of the page and demonstrate as students use individual copies at their seats. Tell students the story map includes all of the elements of a fictional story: characters, setting, problem or conflict, events, and solution or resolution.

Activity #3
Help students fill in the details on the story map. By this time, students have read enough to establish the main character (Scrooge), some minor characters (The Spirit of Christmas Past, Bob Cratchit, the nephew), setting (Christmas Eve, London), problem/conflict (Scrooge is selfish, has no sense of the meaning of the Christmas season), events (the apparition of Marley's ghost, the journey with the first Spirit), and point of view (third person, omniscient speaker.) Tell them to continue filling in information, especially events, as they read. They will complete the map during Lesson 12.

ORAL READING EVALUATION *A Christmas Carol*

Name_____ Class_____ Date_____ - -

SKILL	EXCELLENT	GOOD	AVERAGE	FAIR	POOR
Fluency	5	4	3	2	1
Clarity	5	4	3	2	1
Audibility	5	4	3	2	1
Pronunciation	5	4	3	2	1
_____	5	4	3	2	1
_____	5	4	3	2	1

Total _____ Grade _____

Comments:

LESSON SIX

Student Objectives
    1. To become familiar with the vocabulary for Stave 3
    2. To preview the study questions for Stave 3
    3. To read Stave 3

Activity #1

    Allow about ten minutes for the students to individually complete the prereading vocabulary worksheet for Stave 3.

Activity #2

    Play a game of charades after students have completed the prereading vocabulary worksheet. Arrange students in pairs. Have one member give verbal clues and physical gestures for the word while the other guesses what it is. Do this until all words have been covered.

Activity #3

    Have students preview the study questions for Stave 3 and jot down their answers. Have them compare their answers with those of one or two other students. After they read, have the students get together again and compare the actual answers with those they gave before reading.

Activity #4

    Have students read Stave 3 silently for the remainder of the period. If you have any students who are having difficulty with the reading, you may want to read aloud in a small group with them, stopping frequently to check their understanding.

STORY MAP *A Christmas Carol*

CHARACTERS
Main

Minor

SETTING
Time

Place

THEME

POINT OF VIEW

PROBLEM

EVENTS

SOLUTION

LESSON SEVEN

Student Objectives
    1. To review the main ideas and objectives in Stave 3
    2. To become aware of the differences between American and British spellings

Activity #1

Use an Every Student Response technique to check the answers to the study questions. Distribute four colored strips (1"x3") of paper or index cards to students and have them put the letters A, B, C, D on as follows: A=pink, B=yellow, C=blue, D=green. Read the question and /or show it on the overhead. Have students hold up the card with the letter for the answer they think is correct. You can quickly check and see which students are having difficulties. Remind students to make any necessary corrections on their study sheets.

Activity #2

Write the words *odours, recognising,* and *waggons* on the board, one under the other. Ask students to pronounce them. Ask students if they notice anything different or unusual about the words. Explain that although English is the common language in both the United States and Great Britain, some words are spelled slightly differently. Invite students to explore the words and find the differences. (*odours-odors; recognising-recognizing; waggons-wagons*). Distribute copies of the American/British Spelling Chart (included). Allow students to work with partners to find the American English spellings of the given words. Suggest that they use dictionaries to check their answers. Have them generalize about the changes in the spelling patterns.

Activity #3

Spelling Scavenger Hunt: Provide copies of other Dickens novels and/or writings by other British authors. Have students work in pairs and skim to find more spelling variations. The pair with the most words wins.

Activity #4

British Spelling Bee: Have a spelling bee in which students must spell the words the British way.

BRITISH and AMERICAN ENGLISH SPELLINGS

PAGE	BRITISH SPELLING	AMERICAN SPELLING	DIFFERENCE
7	neighbouring	neighboring	American takes out *u* after *o*
9	humour		
11	endeavouring		
19	vapour		
28	odours		
28	fervour		
28	recognising		
28	travellers		
29	savour		
19	panelling		
32	meagre		
39	defenceless		
42	despatched		
44	demeanour		
45	waggons		
58	offences		
67	skaiter		
69	scrutinise		
74	agonised		
87	endeavour		

LESSON EIGHT

Objectives
To practice writing to persuade

Activity #1
Distribute Writing Assignment #2. Discuss the directions in detail and give students ample time to complete the assignment.

Activity #2
Give students class time to try out their persuasive speeches on each other.

LESSON NINE

Objectives
1. To become familiar with the vocabulary for Stave 4
2. To preview the study questions for Stave 4
3. To read Stave 4
4. To read dialog with expression

Activity #1
Arrange students in groups of three or four. Have them take turns reading each sentence aloud. Then have all group members tell what they think the vocabulary word means, and why they think so. Allow group members to discuss the answers to the matching section as they complete it.

Activity #2
Give students a few minutes to preview the study questions. Then encourage them to add any questions of their own that they want answered.

Activity #3 Activity #3
Invite students to take the parts of the characters and read the chapter aloud.

LESSON TEN

Student Objectives
    1. To participate in a writing conference with the teacher
    2. To revise Writing Assignment #1 based on the teacher's suggestions

Activity #1
    Choose a quiet corner of the room and hold individual writing conferences.

Activity #2
    Students who are not conferencing can either work on revisions of Writing Assignment #1, or begin answering the study questions for Stave Four.

WRITING ASSIGNMENT #2 *A Christmas Carol*
Writing to Persuade

PROMPT
In Stave 1, two businessmen asked Scrooge to donate money to help the poor and destitute. In modern society, this still happens. People are asked, either in person, by telephone, or in writing, to make donations to various causes. You have a favorite charity for which you are raising money. Your assignment is to prepare a persuasive speech to use on your classmates.

PREWRITING
Option 1: Think of a worthwhile charity or organization to which you might like to donate. Find out what the organization does with the money it gets. Then make a list of the reasons someone might be willing to donate money. Think of statements to support each of your reasons, and list them under each reason. Then number the reasons in order from most to least important.

Option 2: Make up a charity or organization. It can be silly or serious. Follow the rest of the directions listed in Option 1.

DRAFTING
Make an introductory statement in which you describe the organization or charity. State your request for a donation.

Use one paragraph for each of your reasons. Use the supporting statements for each reason. Then write a closing statement in which you again ask for a donation.

PEER CONFERENCING/REVISING
When you finish the rough draft, ask another student to look at it. You may want to give the student your checklist so he/she can double check and see that you have included all of the information. After reading, the student should tell you what he or she liked best about your persuasive speech, which parts were difficult to understand or needed more information, and ways in which your work could be improved. Reread your persuasive speech considering your critic's comments and make the revisions you think are necessary.

PROOFREADING/EDITING
Do a final proofreading of your persuasive speech. Double-check your grammar, spelling, organization, and the clarity of your ideas.

FINAL DRAFT
Follow your teacher's guidelines for completing the final draft of your paper.

LESSON ELEVEN

Student Objectives
    1. To review the main ideas and events in Stave 4
    2. To identify adjectives in given sentences from the novel
    3. To correctly use adjectives in original sentences

Activity #1

    Put the numbers 1 through 14 on slips of paper and put them in a dish or small basket. Repeat the numbers as often as necessary to make sure you have one slip of numbered paper for each student in the class. Let each student draw a number until all numbers have been drawn. The student will write the answer for the question on the slip of paper. Then go in order and have students read their questions and answers. If two students have the same number, allow them to each give their answer.

Activity #2 Minilesson: Adjectives

    Distribute blank sheets of paper. Tell the students to draw a dog, a car, or some other common item. Do not give any further directions. After about ten minutes, ask students to hold up their papers and look around at each other's drawings. Comment on the differences. Then give specific directions such as the following and have students draw what you tell them. Have them hold up this drawing and comment on each other's drawings. (These should be more similar.) Ask why the second drawings look so much more alike. If students do not mention the adjectives you used in the description, tell them the drawings look alike because you used adjectives in your description. Remind students that an adjective is a word that modifies, or describes, a noun. Adjectives answer the following questions about nouns: what kind? which? how much? how many? Ask students how an author can use adjectives. Read the suggested passages from the book aloud and invite students to comment on Dickens's use of adjectives.

Directions for drawing: Draw a side view of a large dog. Give it a fat body. Make the dog have a large face with a pointed snout and upright pointed ears. Give the dog large, round eyes.
Put curly fur on the dog. Give the dog a long, straight, thick tail. Make the dog's feet large.

Passages: Stave 1, beginning with, "Oh! but he was a tight-fisted hand at the grindstone. . . . "
        Stave 2: beginning with. "It was a strange figure--like a child. . . . "
        Stave 3: beginning with, "It was his own room."

Activity #3

    Distribute copies of the adjective chart and go over the directions. Have students work individually to complete the adjective chart. You may want to assign a particular chapter or group of pages for each individual or small group. When they are finished, have students work in small groups to compare their findings. Collect the papers and review them for accuracy.

Activity #4

    Ask students to apply what they have learned about using adjectives by writing a description of a real or imaginary character, then illustrating their description. Display their work on a bulletin board.

ADJECTIVE CHART

Directions: Read through the assigned pages of *A Christmas Carol* to find the adjectives. Write the adjective and the noun it modifies. Underline the adjective. Then check off the type of adjective in the appropriate column. A sample from the first page has been done for you.

ADJECTIVE and NOUN	What kind	Which	How many	How much
<u>sad</u> event	X			

Write a description of a real or imaginary character. Draw a picture of it on the back.

LESSON TWELVE

Objectives
1. To become familiar with the vocabulary for Stave 5
2. To preview the study questions for Stave 5
3. To read Stave 5
4. To discuss the main ideas and events in Stave 5
5. To complete the story chart
6. To discuss the character development of Scrooge

Activity #1
Give students about fifteen minutes to complete the vocabulary worksheet and go over the study guide questions.

Activity #2 Minilesson: Character Development
Before reading, ask students what they think will happen to Scrooge now that he has been visited by all three Spirits, and if he will change. Have students skim through the first four staves to find examples of Scrooge's character and behaviors. Then have them find examples of changes in Stave 5. You may want to have students record their responses on the included chart.

Activity #3
Read the last stave aloud, or have students read it silently.

Activity #4
Discuss students' predictions. Then discuss the study guide questions, and have students write down the answers as you discuss them.

Activity #5
Work with students to complete the story map.

SCROOGE'S CHARACTER
A Christmas Carol

BEFORE	THE SAME	AFTER

Draw a picture of Scrooge before the visits from the Spirits, and one of him after the visits.

LESSON THIRTEEN

Objective
To discuss *A Christmas Carol* at the interpretive and critical levels

Activity #1
Choose the questions from the Extra Writing Assignments/Discussion Questions which seem most appropriate for your students. A class discussion of these questions is most effective if students have been given the opportunity to formulate answers to the questions prior to the discussion. To this end, you may either have all the students formulate answers to all the questions, divide the class into groups and assign one or more questions to each group, or you could assign one questions to each student in your class. The option you choose will make a difference in the amount of class time needed for this activity.

Activity #2
After students have had ample time to formulate answers to the questions, begin your class discussion of the questions and the ideas presented by the questions. Be sure students take notes during the discussion so they have information to study for the unit test.

EXTRA WRITING ASSIGNMENT/ DISCUSSION QUESTIONS
A Christmas Carol

Interpretive
1. From what point of view is the novel written? How does this affect your understanding of the story?

2. Discuss the main themes in the novel.

3. Discuss the changes in Scrooge during the course of the novel.

4. The story said that Marley had died seven years earlier. Was there any significance to Dickens using the number 7?

5. Discuss the symbolism of the chains on Marley's ghost.

6. Why did Scrooge leave Marley's name on the door, even though Marley was dead?

7. How do you think Bob Cratchit felt about working for Scrooge? Why do you think he stayed there?

8. What were Marley's chains and Scrooge's chains made of?

9. The narrator used the words Ghost, Spirit, and Phantom to describe the visitors. How did this affect your understanding and enjoyment of the novel?

10. In Stave 3, the narrator calls Dickens the Ogre of the Cratchit family. How does Dickens show this to be true?

11. In Stave 3, what do you think Scrooge was thinking when he left the Cratchit home?

12. In Stave 3, how do you think Scrooge felt when he discovered he was the topic of the Yes/No game?

13. In Stave 4, why didn't Scrooge realize at first that he was the dead man the others were talking about?

14. When did Scrooge first become aware of the way that others saw him?

Critical

15. Why didn't the Ghost of Christmas Yet to Come speak to Scrooge?

16. Why didn't Dickens name the clerk in Stave 1? Why did he wait until Stave 2 to do so?

17. The year in which the novel takes place is not given. How can you, the reader, tell approximately when the story took place?

18. How important is the year to the plot? Could the plot work in another time and place?

19. What does Scrooge's choice of a place to live tell about him?

20. Discuss the author's style. How does Dickens keep the reader's interest? Does he use symbolism effectively?

21. In the beginning of the novel, Marley's ghost tells Scrooge the Spirits will appear on three consecutive nights. When Scrooge awakes, it is Christmas Day, and he comments that the spirits have done their work in just one night Why do you think Dickens had the events occur this way?

22. Why did Dickens include the scene in Stave 4 with the laundress, the charwoman, and the undertaker's assistant?

23. What was the purpose of Marley's Ghost? Would the story have been as effective if Dickens had only used the three Spirits?

Personal Response

24. How did you feel about Scrooge at the beginning of the story? How did you feel at the end? If your feelings changed, why?

25. Do you think Scrooge really saw the Spirits, or was it a dream?

26. How did the setting affect your enjoyment of the novel?

27. How did the use of an omniscient narrator affect your understanding of the story?

28. If you were Bob Cratchit, what would you think about Scrooge and his behavior on the day after Christmas?

29. Which of the characters did you like, and why?

30. Which of the characters did you dislike, and why?

31. Which scene in the story did you like most? Why?

32. Was the title effective? Why or why not?

33. What other title would you choose for this book?

34. Would you recommend this book to a friend? Why or why not?

35. Did you like the ending of the novel? Why or why not?

36. Which of the scenes Scrooge saw with the Spirits affected him the most?

37. How do you think Scrooge spent the next Christmas, after the story ended?

38. Why do you think Scrooge acted the way he did at the beginning of the story?

39. Which episode do you think had the greatest effect on Scrooge? Why?

40. If you had a chain like Marley's what would it look like?

QUOTATIONS *A Christmas Carol*

Discuss the significance of the following quotations.

1. Marley was dead, to begin with. There is no doubt whatever about that.

2. "Bah! Humbug!"

3. "I wish to be left alone," said Scrooge. "Since you ask me what I wish, gentlemen, that is my answer. I don't make merry myself at Christmas, and I can't afford to make idle people merry. I help to support the establishments I have mentioned; they cost enough: and those who are badly off must go there."

4. "It's not my business," Scrooge returned. "It's enough for a man to understand his own business, and not to interfere with other people's. Mine occupies me constantly. Good afternoon, gentlemen!"

5. "It is required of every man," the Ghost returned, "that the spirit within him should walk abroad among his fellow-men, and travel far and wide; and if that spirit goes not forth in life, it is condemned to do so after death. It is doomed to wander through the world--oh, woe is me! --and witness what it cannot share, but might have shared on earth, and turned to happiness!"

6. "I wear the chain I forged in life," replied the Ghost. "I made it link by link, and yard by yard; I girded it on of my own free will, and of my own free will I wore it. Is its pattern strange to you?"

7. "Or would you know," pursued the Ghost, "the weight and length of the strong coil you bear yourself? It was full and heavy and as long as this, seven Christmas Eves ago. You have labored on it, since. It is a ponderous chain!"

8. "I have none to give," the Ghost replied. "It comes from other regions, Ebenezer Scrooge, and is conveyed by other ministers, to other kinds of men. Nor can I tell you what I would. A very little more is all permitted to me. I cannot rest, I cannot stay, I cannot linger anywhere. My sprit never walked beyond our counting house--mark me!--in life my spirit never roved beyond the narrow limits of our money-changing hole; and weary journeys lie before me!"

9. "What!" exclaimed the Ghost, "would you so soon put out, with worldly hands, the light I give? Is it not enough that you are one of those whose passions made this cap, and force me through whole trains of years to wear it low upon my brow!"

10. "The school is not quite deserted," said the Ghost. "A solitary child, neglected by his friends, is left there still."

11. "Home, little Fan?" returned the boy.

12. "It isn't that, Spirit. He has the power to render us happy or unhappy; to make our service light or burdensome; a pleasure or a toil. Say that his power lies in words and looks; in things so slight and insignificant that it is impossible to add and count 'em up; what then? The happiness he gives, is quite as great as if it cost a fortune."

13. "You fear the world too much," she answered, gently. "All your other hopes have merged into the hope of being beyond the chance of its sordid reproach. I have seen your nobler aspirations fall off one by one, until the master-passion, Gain, engrosses you. Have I not?"

14. ". . . I release you. With a full heart, for the love of him you once were."

15. "Belle," said the husband, turning to his wife with a smile. "I saw an old friend of yours this afternoon."

16. "Spirit," said Scrooge submissively, "conduct me where you will. I went forth last night on compulsion, and I learnt a lesson which is working now. To-night, if you have aught to teach me, let me profit by it."

17. "Spirit," said Scrooge, after a moment's thought," I wonder you, of all the beings in the many worlds about us, should desire to cramp these people's opportunities of innocent enjoyment."

18. "There are some upon this earth of yours," returned the Spirit, "who lay claim to know us, and who do their deeds of passion, pride, ill-will, hatred, envy, bigotry, and selfishness in our name, who are as strange to us and all our kith and kin, as if they had never lived. Remember that, and charge their doings on themselves, not us."

19. "As good as gold," said Bob, "and better. Somehow he gets thoughtful sitting by himself so much, and thinks the strangest things you ever heard. He told me, coming home, that he hoped the people saw him in the church, because he was a cripple, and it might be pleasant to them to remember upon Christmas Day, who made lame beggars walk and blind men see."

20. "God bless us every one!" said Tiny Tim, the last of all.

21. "Man," said the Ghost, "if man you be in heart, not adamant, forbear that wicked cant until you have discovered What the surplus is, and Where it is. Will you decide what men shall live, what men shall die? It may be, that in the sight of Heaven, you are more worthless and less fit to live than millions like this poor man's child. Oh god! to hear the Insect on the leaf pronouncing on the too much life among his hungry brothers in the dust!"

22. "I'll drink his health for your sake and the Day's," said Mrs. Cratchit, "not for his."

23. "He's a comical old fellow," said Scrooge's nephew, "that's the truth; and not so pleasant as he might be. However, his offences carry their own punishment, and I have nothing to say against him."

24. "I have found it out! I know what it is, Fred! I know what it is!"
    "What is it?" cried Fred?
    "It's your Uncle Scro-o-o-oge!"

25. Scrooge started back, appalled. Having them shown to him in this way, he tried to say they were fine children, but the words choked themselves, rather than be parties to a lie of such enormous magnitude.

26. "Ghost of the future!" he exclaimed, "I fear you more than any Spectre I have seen. But as I know your purpose is to do me good, and as I hope to live to be another man form what I was, I am prepared to bear you company, and do it with a thankful heart. Will you not speak to me?"

27. "If he wanted to keep 'em after he was dead, a wicked old screw," pursued the woman, "why wasn't he natural in his lifetime? If he had been, he'd have had somebody to look after him when he was struck with Death, instead of lying gasping out his last there, alone by himself."

28. "I certainly shan't hold my hand, when I get anything in it by reaching it out, for the sake of such a man as He was, I promise you, Joe," returned the woman coolly.

29. "This is the end of it, you see! He frightened every one way from him when he was alive, to profit us when he was dead! Ha, ha, ha."

30. Oh cold, cold, rigid, dreadful Death, set up thine altar here, and dress it with such terrors as thou hast at thy command: for this is thy dominion! But of the loved, revered, and honoured dead, thou canst not turn one hair to thy dread purposes, or make one feature odious. It is not that the hand is heavy and will fall down when released; it is not that the heart and pulse are still; but that the hand WAS open, generous, and true; the heart brave, warm, and tender; and the pulse a man's. Strike, Shadow, strike! And see his good deeds springing from the wound, to sow the world with life immortal!

31. " I hope they do. 'Heartily sorry,' he said, 'for your good wife. If I can be of any service to you in any way,' he said, giving me his card, 'that's where I live. Pray come to me.' Now, it wasn't," cried Bob, "for the sake of anything he might be able to do for us, so much as for his kind way, that this was quite delightful. It really seemed as if he had known our Tiny Tim, and felt with us."

32. "Men's courses will foreshadow certain ends, to which, if persevered in, they must lead," said Scrooge. "But if the courses be departed from, the ends will change. Say it is thus with what you show me!"

33. "I will live in the Past, the Present, and the Future!" Scrooge repeated, as he scrambled out of bed. "The Spirits of all Three shall strive within me. Oh Jacob Marley! Heaven, and the Christmas Time be praised for this! I say it on my knees, old Jacob, on my knees!"

LESSON FOURTEEN

Objective
  To review all of the vocabulary work done in this unit

VOCABULARY REVIEW ACTIVITIES

1. Divide your class into two teams and have an old-fashioned spelling or definition bee.

2. Give each of your students (or students in groups of two, three or four) a Vocabulary Word Search Puzzle for *A Christmas Carol*. The person (group) to find all of the vocabulary words in the puzzle first wins.

3. Give students a vocabulary Word Search Puzzle for *A Christmas Carol* without the word list. The person or group to find the most vocabulary words in the puzzle wins.

4. Use a Vocabulary Crossword Puzzle for *A Christmas Carol*. Put the puzzle onto a transparency on the overhead projector (so everyone can see it), and do the puzzle together as a class.

5. Give students a Vocabulary Matching Worksheet to do.

6. Divide your class into two teams. Use the *A Christmas Carol* vocabulary words with their letters jumbled as a word list. Student 1 from Team A faces off against Student 1 from Team B. You write the first jumbled word on the board. The first student (1A or 1B) to unscramble the word wins the chance for his/her team to score points. If 1A wins the jumble, go to student 2A and give him/her a definition. He/she must give you the correct spelling of the vocabulary word which fits that definition. If he/she does, Team A scores a point, and you give student 3A a definition for which you expect a correctly spelled matching vocabulary word. Continue giving Team A definitions until some team member makes an incorrect response. An incorrect response sends the game back to the jumbled-word face off, this time with students 2A and 2B. Instead of repeating giving definitions to the first few students of each team, continue with the student after the one who gave the last incorrect response on the team. For example, if Team B wins the jumbled-word face-off, and student 5B gave the last incorrect answer for Team B, you would start this round of definition questions with student 6B, and so on. The team with the most points wins!

7. Have students write a story in which they correctly use as many vocabulary words as possible. Have students read their compositions orally. Post the most original compositions on your bulletin board!

LESSON FIFTEEN

Objective
>To review the main ideas presented in *A Christmas Carol*

Activity #1
>Choose one of the review games/activities included in the packet and spend your class period as outlined there.

Activity #2
>Remind students of the date for the Unit Test. Stress the review of the Study Guides and their class notes as a last minute, brush-up review for homework.

REVIEW GAMES / ACTIVITIES

1. Ask the class to make up a unit test for *A Christmas Carol*. The test should have 4 sections: multiple choice, true/false, short answer and essay. Students may use 1/2 period to make the test, including a separate answer sheet, and then swap papers and use the other 1/2 class period to take a test a classmate has devised. (open book)

2. Take 1/2 period for students to make up true and false questions (including the answers). Collect the papers and divide the class into two teams. Draw a big tic-tac-toe board on the chalk board. Make one team X and one team O. Ask questions to each side, giving each student one turn. If the question is answered correctly, that student's team's letter (X or O) is placed in the box. If the answer is incorrect, no mark is placed in the box. The object is to get three marks in a row like tic-tac-toe. You may want to keep track of the number of games won for each team.

3. Take 1/2 period for students to make up questions (true/false and short answer). Collect the questions. Divide the class into two teams. You'll alternate asking questions to individual members of teams A & B (like in a spelling bee). The question keeps going from A to B until it is correctly answered, then a new question is asked. A correct answer does not allow the team to get another question. Correct answers are +2 points; incorrect answers are -1 point.

4. Allow students time to quiz each other (in pairs) from their study guides and class notes.

5. Give students a crossword puzzle from *A Christmas Carol* to complete.

6. Divide your class into two teams. Use the *A Christmas Carol* crossword words with their letters jumbled as a word list. Student 1 from Team A faces off against Student 1 from Team B. You write the first jumbled word on the board. The first student (1A or 1B) to unscramble the word wins the chance for his/her team to score points. If 1A wins the jumble, go to student 2A and give him/her a clue. He/she must give you the correct word which matches that clue. If he/she does, Team A scores a point, and you give student 3A a clue for which you expect another correct response. Continue giving Team A clues until some team member makes an incorrect response. An incorrect response sends the game back to the jumbled-word face off, this time with students 2A and 2B. Instead of repeating giving clues to the first few students of each team, continue with the student after the one who gave the last incorrect response on the team.

7. Take on the persona of "The Answer Person." Allow students to ask any question about the book. Answer the questions, or tell students where to look in the book to find the answer.

8. Students may enjoy playing charades with events from the story. Select a student to start. Give him/her a card with a scene or event from the story. Allow the players to use their books to find the scene being described. The first person to guess each charade performs the next one.

9. Play a categories-type quiz game. (A master is included in this Unit Plan). Make an overhead transparency of the categories form. Divide the class into teams of three or four players each. Have each team choose a recorder and a banker. Choose a team to go first. That team will choose a category and point amount. Ask the question to the entire class.(Use the Study Guide Quiz and Vocabulary questions.) Give the teams one minute to discuss the answer and write it down. Walk around the room and check the answers. Each team that answers correctly receives the points. (Incorrect answers are not penalized; they just don't receive any points). Cross out that square on the playing board. Play continues until all squares have been used. The winning team is the one with the most points. You can assign bonus points to any square or squares you choose.

10. Have students complete the last column (What I Learned) of the KWL sheet you distributed in Lesson One. Discuss their answers with the class.

QUIZ GAME
A Christmas Carol

Stave 1　　Marley's Ghost	Stave 2　　The First of the Three Spirits	Stave 3　　The Second of the Three Spirits	Stave 4　　The Last of the Spirits	Stave 5　　The End of It
100	100	100	100	100
200	200	200	200	200
300	300	300	300	300
400	400	400	400	400
500	500	500	500	500

LESSON SIXTEEN

Objective
To test the students' understanding of the main ideas and themes in *A Christmas Carol*

Activity #1
Distribute the *A Christmas Carol* Unit Tests. Go over the instructions in detail and allow the students the entire class period to complete the exam.

Activity #2
Collect all test papers and assigned books prior to the end of the class period.

NOTES ABOUT THE UNIT TESTS IN THIS UNIT:

There are 5 different unit tests which follow.

There are two short answer tests which are based primarily on facts from the novel. The answer key for Short Answer Unit Test 1 follows the student test. The answer key for Short Answer Test 2 follows the student Short Answer Unit Test 2.

There is one advanced short answer unit test. It is based on the extra discussion questions. Use the matching key for short answer unit test 2 to check the matching section of the advanced short answer unit test. There is no key for the short answer questions. The answers will be based on the discussions you have had during class.

There are two multiple choice unit tests. Following the two unit tests, you will find an answer sheet on which students should mark their answers. The same answer sheet should be used for both tests; however, students' answers will be different for each test. Following the students' answer sheet for the multiple choice tests you will find your answer keys.

The short answer tests have a vocabulary section. You should choose 20 of the vocabulary words from this unit, read them orally and have the students write them down. Then, either have students write a definition or use the words in sentences.

LESSON SEVENTEEN

Objectives
1. To widen the breadth of students' knowledge about the topics discussed or touched upon in *A Christmas Carol*
2. To check students' non-fiction assignments

Activity

Ask each student to give a brief oral report about the nonfiction work he/she read for the nonfiction assignment. Your criteria for evaluating this report will vary depending on the level of your students. You may wish for students to give a complete report without using notes of any kind, or you may want students to read directly from a written report, or you may want to do something in between these two extremes. Just make students aware of your criteria in ample time for them to prepare their reports.

Start with one student's report. After that, ask if anyone else in the class has read on a topic related to the first student's report. If no one has, choose another student at random. After each report, be sure to ask if anyone has a report related to the one just completed. That will help keep a continuity during the discussion of the reports.

LESSON EIGHTEEN

Student Objective

To practice writing to express a personal opinion

Activity #1

Distribute copies of Writing Assignment #3 and go over it with the students.
Give them the rest of the class period to work on the assignment. If they need extra time, assign a due date.

Activity #2

Invite willing students to share their opinion papers with the class.

WRITING ASSIGNMENT # 3 *A Christmas Carol*
Writing to Express a Personal Opinion

PROMPT
At the end of Stave 5, the narrator states that Scrooge "knew how to keep Christmas well, if any man possessed the knowledge." What do you think it means to "keep Christmas well"? Your assignment is to write your opinion of how to celebrate Christmas. If you do not celebrate Christmas, think of another holiday you do observe, and write about ways to truly keep in the spirit of the holiday. If you do not celebrate any holidays, write about how people should treat one another in daily life.

PREWRITING
Make a web or brainstorm list of your ideas. Then organize them into groups that go together. Make sure each idea has supporting details or examples to go along with it. Decide on the order in which you want to present your ideas, and number them.

DRAFTING
In the first paragraph, introduce your holiday and state the purpose of your paper. In the following paragraphs, present your ideas. Use the supporting details or examples to explain each of your ideas. In the closing paragraph, re-state your purpose.

PEER CONFERENCING/REVISING
When you finish the rough draft, ask another student to look at it. After reading, the student should tell you what he or she liked best about your opinion paper, which parts were difficult to understand or needed more information, and ways in which your work could be improved. Reread your paper considering your critic's comments and make the revisions you think are necessary.

PROOFREADING/EDITING
Do a final proofreading of your opinion paper. Double-check your grammar, spelling, organization, and the clarity of your ideas.

FINAL DRAFT
Follow your teacher's guidelines for completing the final draft of your paper.

LESSON NINETEEN

Student Objectives
1. To watch a movie version of the novel *A Christmas Carol*
2. To compare and contrast the movie with the book
3. To listen to an audio version of the novel
4. To compare and contrast the audio version with the book

Activity #1
The movie version of *A Christmas Carol* is available in many video stores, and through educational film distributors. Show the movie in class.

Activity #2
Discuss the ways in which the movie and the novel were similar and different. Discuss the reasons for the differences. You may want the students to draw and complete a Venn Diagram and/or write a short comparison/contrast paper after this discussion.

Activity #3
Several audio versions of *A Christmas Carol* are available. You may want to have students listen instead of, or in addition to, watching the movie. Discuss the similarities and differences between the two versions.

LESSON TWENTY

Student Objective
1. To complete Project Tiny Tim
2. To evaluate the effectiveness of Project Tiny Tim

Activity #1
Allow students time to complete their projects, or use the time to take a field trip to the location the students chose for the project.

Activity #2
Involve students in a discussion of their project. What went well? Where could they have improved, and how? Did they think the project was successful?

Activity #3
Give students time to write thank-you notes to anyone who helped with the project.

UNIT TESTS

SHORT ANSWER UNIT TEST 1 *A Christmas Carol*

I. Matching/ Identify

___ 1.	Bob Cratchit	A.	showed people toasting Scrooge's health
___ 2.	Spirit of Christmas Past	B.	had the power to make others happy or unhappy
___ 3.	Spirit of Christmas Present	C.	invited Scrooge to Christmas dinner
___ 4.	Christmas Yet to Come	D.	might die in future if present didn't change
___ 5.	Tiny Tim	E.	clerk and family man
___ 6.	nephew	F.	covetous old sinner
___ 7.	Jacob Marley	G.	thought Scrooge loved money more than her
___ 8.	Ebenezer Scrooge	H.	came to aid Scrooge's welfare and reclamation
___ 9.	Fezziwig	I.	wore the chains he forged in life
___ 10.	Belle	J.	showed scene of a dead man who was not mourned

II. Short Answer

1. Who appeared to Scrooge first? What did he tell Scrooge?

2. Describe the first scene Scrooge and the Spirit of Christmas Past visited. How did Scrooge feel about what he saw?

Short Answer Unit Test 1 *A Christmas Carol*

3. Describe Scrooge and the Spirit of Christmas Present's visit to Scrooge's nephew's house. What did Scrooge's nephew and nieces say about him? What did Scrooge think about when he heard the harp music? What did Scrooge do while his nephew and the others were playing games? Describe the "Yes and No" game. What was the subject of the game? How did Scrooge feel by the time he and the Spirit left his nephew's house?

4. How did Scrooge feel about the Ghost of Christmas Yet to Come? What did the Ghost of Christmas Yet to Come look like? Where did Scrooge and the Spirit go first? What did they see and hear?

5. How did Scrooge act when he went outside after he had been visited by the Spirits?

Short Answer Unit Test 1 *A Christmas Carol*

III. <u>Fill-In-The Blank</u>   Directions: Use a word or a phrase to complete each sentence about the story.

1. The story took place in _____ on a Christmas Eve and Christmas Day.

2. On Christmas Eve night, the ghost of _____, Scrooge's dead business partner, visited him.

3. The Spirit of Christmas _____ was the first to visit Scrooge.

4. This Spirit took Scrooge to see _____. (Name any one of the four visits.)

5. The second Spirit was _____.

6. This Spirit took Scrooge to see people happily celebrating Christmas. One place they visited was _____. (Name any one of the places they visited.)

7. The second Spirit told Scrooge that if things did not change in the future, a lame and sickly child named _____ might die. This disturbed Scrooge.

8. The third Spirit was _____.

9. This Spirit showed Scrooge his own _____.

10. Scrooge was a changed man when he woke up on Christmas Day. One of the new and different things he did was _____.
    (Name any one of the things he did.)

Short Answer Unit Test 1 *A Christmas Carol*

IV. <u>Essay</u>

How did Scrooge change from the beginning to the end of the story?
What events helped cause these changes?

Short Answer Unit Test 1 *A Christmas Carol*

V. Vocabulary

Listen to the vocabulary words and spell them. After you have spelled all the words, go back and write down the definitions.

WORD	**DEFINITION**
1. _____	_____
2. _____	_____
3. _____	_____
4. _____	_____
5. _____	_____
6. _____	_____
7. _____	_____
8. _____	_____
9. _____	_____
10. _____	_____

Vocabulary Part 2   Place the letter of the matching definition on the blank line.

_____ 1. benevolence   A. comfort; compassion
_____ 2. consolation   B. protested
_____ 3. cordially   C. avaricious; greedy; eagerly desirous of
_____ 4. covetous   D. notoriously bad
_____ 5. destitute   E. generosity; kindness
_____ 6. illustrious   F. easily influenced; susceptible
_____ 7. infamous   G. graciously; in a friendly way
_____ 8. odious   H. glorious; brilliant
_____ 9. remonstrated   I. hateful
_____ 10. susceptible   J. poor; penniless

ANSWER KEY SHORT ANSWER UNIT TEST 1 *A Christmas Carol*

1. Matching/ Identify

E	1.	Bob Cratchit	A.	showed people toasting Scrooge's health
H	2.	Spirit of Christmas Past	B.	had the power to make others happy or unhappy
A	3.	Spirit of Christmas Present	C.	invited Scrooge to Christmas dinner
J	4.	Christmas Yet to Come	D.	might die in future if present didn't change
D	5.	Tiny Tim	E.	clerk and family man
C	6.	nephew	F.	covetous old sinner
I	7.	Jacob Marley	G.	thought Scrooge loved money more than her
F	8.	Ebenezer Scrooge	H.	came to aid Scrooge's welfare and reclamation
B	9.	Fezziwig	I.	wore the chains he forged in life
G	10.	Belle	J.	showed scene of a dead man who was not mourned

II. Short Answer

1. Who appeared to Scrooge first? What did he tell Scrooge?

    Marley's ghost appeared. He told Scrooge he was doomed to travel the world forever and look at all of the kindness and happiness he had missed. The chains he wore were ones he had made himself when he was alive. He said Scrooge was headed on the same path, and had a chain even longer than his own. He also said Scrooge still had a chance to redeem himself.

2. Describe the first scene Scrooge and the Spirit of Christmas Past visited. How did Scrooge feel about what he saw?

    It was Scrooge's boyhood home and school. They saw Scrooge as a young boy, reading. At first Scrooge seemed excited. Then he seemed to pity his former self. Then he said he wished he had given something to the young boy who had been singing at his door the night before.

3. Describe Scrooge and the Spirit of Christmas Present's visit to Scrooge's nephew's house. What did Scrooge's nephew and nieces say about him? What did Scrooge think about when he heard the harp music? What did Scrooge do while his nephew and the others were playing games? Describe the "Yes and No" game. What was the subject of the game? How did Scrooge feel by the time he and the Spirit left his nephew's house?

    His nephew thought Scrooge was a "comical old fellow." He said he felt sorry for Scrooge, that he was the one who really suffered for his own ill whims. Scrooge's niece and the other women said they had no patience with him.

    Scrooge thought that if he could have listened to the harp music more when he was younger, he might have been able to be kinder.

Scrooge joined in the games, even though the others couldn't see or hear him.

Scrooge's nephew thought of something, and the rest had to find out what it was by asking questions that could be answered either "yes" or "no." Clues were that it was a live, disagreeable animal that lived in London. One of the nieces guessed that it was Scrooge.

Scrooge was cheerful and light-hearted when he and the Spirit left. He thanked them, although his thanks was not heard.

4. How did Scrooge feel about the Ghost of Christmas Yet to Come? What did the Ghost of Christmas Yet to Come look like? Where did Scrooge and the Spirit go first? What did they see and hear? How did Scrooge feel about being with this Spirit?

He feared this Ghost. His legs trembled, and he could hardly stand up.

It was covered by a black garment. It was tall, and did not speak.

They went to the city first. While there, they saw several businessmen. They were discussing another businessman's (Old Scratch) death and what he had done with his money. They also wondered who would go to his funeral, since none of them liked him and he had no friends. Although Scrooge was afraid of the Spirit, he knew he would learn something for his own improvement. He treasured everything he heard and saw.

5. How did Scrooge act when he went outside after he had been visited by the Spirits?

He was smiling and saying hello to people. He saw one of the business men who had asked him for a donation the day before. He whispered an amount in the man's ear and asked the man to come and see him.

III. <u>Fill-In-The Blank</u>

1. The story took place in **London** on a Christmas Eve and Christmas Day.
2. On Christmas Eve night, the ghost of **Jacob Marley**, Scrooge's dead business partner, visited him.
3. The Spirit of Christmas **Past** was the first to visit Scrooge.
4. This Spirit took Scrooge to see **his childhood home and school, his sister, Fan, his former master Fezziwig, his former fiancée Belle.** (Name any one of the four visits.)
5. The second Spirit was **The Spirit of Christmas Present**.
6. This Spirit took Scrooge to see people happily celebrating Christmas. One place they visited was the **Cratchit family, his nephew's family, the miners, a lighthouse, a ship.** (Name any one of the places they visited.)
7. The second Spirit told Scrooge that if things did not change in the future, his clerk's lame and sickly child named **Tiny Tim** might die. This disturbed Scrooge.
8. The third Spirit was **The Spirit of Christmas Yet to Come**.
9. This Spirit showed Scrooge his own **death, tomb stone**.
10. Scrooge was a changed man when he woke up on Christmas Day. One of the new and different things he did was **send a turkey to the Cratchit family, have dinner with his nephew, give Bob Cratchit a raise, buy another coal scuttle, become like a second father to Tiny Tim.**. (Name any one of the things he did.)

V. <u>Vocabulary</u> Choose ten of the vocabulary words to dictate for this section of the test.

Vocabulary Part 2

E	1.	benevolence	A.	comfort; compassion
A	2.	consolation	B.	protested
G	3.	cordially	C.	avaricious; greedy; eagerly desirous of
C	4.	covetous	D.	notoriously bad
J	5.	destitute	E.	generosity; kindness
H	6.	illustrious	F.	easily influenced; susceptible
D	7.	infamous	G.	graciously; in a friendly way
I	8.	odious	H.	glorious; brilliant
B	9.	remonstrated	I.	hateful
F	10.	susceptible	J.	poor; penniless

SHORT ANSWER UNIT TEST 2 *A Christmas Carol*

I. Matching/ Identify

____ 1. "Bah! Humbug!"   A. Scrooge's reply to his nephew's dinner invitation
____ 2. Ignorance   B. Tiny Tim's toast
____ 3. "Good Afternoon!"   C. businessmen's nickname for the dead man
____ 4. Want   D. Scrooge's response to "Merry Christmas."
____ 5. Bob Cratchit   E. took the dead Scrooge's sheets and towels
____ 6. "God bless us, everyone."   F. written on the boy's face
____ 7. Doom   G. the girl under the Spirit's robe
____ 8. Mrs. Dilber   H. Scrooge's sister
____ 9. Old Scratch   I. the boy under the Spirit's robe
____ 10. Fan   J. Scrooge's clerk

II. Short Answer

1. Describe the scene at Scrooge's warehouse on Christmas Eve day. Tell who was there, what they wanted, and how Scrooge replied.

2. Describe the scene with Belle.

Short Answer Unit Test 2 *A Christmas Carol*

3. Describe Marley's ghost and all of the three Spirits. Tell what they wore and what they were called.

4. Describe the visit to Bob Cratchit's home that Scrooge and The Spirit of Christmas Present made.

5. The Ghost of Christmas Yet To Come took Scrooge to the city. Describe what they saw in the city. Do not include the visit to Bob Cratchit's house.

Short Answer Unit Test 2 *A Christmas Carol*

III. Fill-In-The-Blank   Directions: Use a word or a phrase to complete each sentence about the story.

1. Ebenezer Scrooge didn't like to celebrate _____.

2. When his nephew invited him to _____, he refused.

3. Ebenezer didn't want to give his clerk a _____.

4. Scrooge's dead business partner, _____, appeared to him and told him he needed to change.

5. The Spirit of Christmas _____ took Scrooge to see his boyhood home and school.

6. The Spirit of Christmas Present took Scrooge to see people who were _____.

7. The Spirit of Christmas _____ told Scrooge that if things did not change in the future, his clerk's lame son, Tiny Tim, might die.

8. The Spirit of Christmas _____ showed Scrooge three people in a dirty shop.

9. These people had _____.

10. Scrooge was a changed man when he woke up on Christmas Day. One of the new and different things he did was _____ (Name any one of the things he did.)

IV. Essay

Discuss the main themes of the novel.

Short Answer Unit Test 2 *A Christmas Carol*

V. Vocabulary

Listen to the vocabulary words and spell them. After you have spelled all the words, go back and write down the definitions.

WORD	DEFINITION
1. _____	_____
2. _____	_____
3. _____	_____
4. _____	_____
5. _____	_____
6. _____	_____
7. _____	_____
8. _____	_____
9. _____	_____
10. _____	_____

Vocabulary Part 2 Place the letter of the matching definition on the blank line.

_____ 1. alteration   A. very bad; offensive
_____ 2. blithe   B. humorous; merry
_____ 3. capacious   C. sadness; depression; gloom
_____ 4. disdaining   D. spacious; large
_____ 5. execrable   E. being everywhere
_____ 6. facetious   F. treating with scorn or contempt
_____ 7. inexorable   G. repaid
_____ 8. melancholy   H. relentless; unyielding
_____ 9. recompensed   I. joyous; happy
_____ 10. ubiquitous   J. change

ANSWER KEY SHORT ANSWER UNIT TEST 2 *A Christmas Carol*

I. <u>Matching/ Identify: Also use this key for the Advanced Short Answer Test.</u>

D	1.	"Bah! Humbug!"	A.	Scrooge's reply to his nephew's dinner invitation
I	2.	Ignorance	B.	Tiny Tim's toast
A	3.	"Good Afternoon!"	C.	released Scrooge from his promise of marriage
G	4.	Want	D.	Scrooge's response to "Merry Christmas."
J	5.	Bob Cratchit	E.	took the dead Scrooge's sheets and towels
B	6.	"God bless us, everyone."	F.	written on the boy's face
F	7.	Doom	G.	the girl under the Spirit's robe
E	8.	Mrs. Dilber	H.	Scrooge's sister
C	9.	Belle	I.	the boy under the Spirit's robe
H	10.	Fan	J.	Scrooge's clerk

II. <u>Short Answer</u>

1. Describe the scene at Scrooge's warehouse on Christmas Eve day. Tell who was there, what they wanted, and how Scrooge replied.

    Scrooge's nephew came to wish him a merry Christmas and invite him for Christmas dinner. Scrooge said he did not think keeping Christmas had ever helped his nephew. He asked the nephew why he had married. He replied only "Good Afternoon" when the nephew invited Scrooge to dinner.

    Some businessmen came to talk to Scrooge. They asked for a donation for the poor and destitute. Scrooge replied that he did not make merry, and could not afford to help idle people make merry.

    Scrooge told his clerk, Bob Cratchit, he thought it was unfair that he should pay the man a day's wages for a day he was not working. He was also annoyed that the clerk wanted the whole day off.

2. Describe the scene with Belle.

    Belle was a young woman to whom Scrooge was apparently engaged. She told him she was releasing him from his promise to marry her. She felt that money and gain were more important to him than she was. Later Scrooge saw her with her husband and family. Her husband mentioned that he had seen Scrooge sitting alone in his office. At that point, Scrooge asked the Ghost to take him away.

3. Describe Marley's ghost and all of the three Spirits. Give their names and what they looked like.

   Marley's ghost was transparent. It wore the clothes Jacob Marley had worn when alive. The chain was made of cash boxes, ledgers, keys, and purses. It wore a folded kerchief around its head and chin.
   The first Spirit was the Spirit of Christmas Present. It was like a child and an old man at the same time. It had long white hair and a face without wrinkles. Its arms and legs were long and strong. The Spirit wore a white tunic trimmed with summer flowers. Its belt sparkled and glimmered in different parts. There was a jet of light coming from the crown of its head. It held a branch of green holly in one hand. It was the Ghost of Christmas Past.
   The second Spirit was the Ghost of Christmas Present. It wore a green robe with a white fur border. It had bare feet, and wore a holly wreath over its long, brown curls.
   The Ghost of Christmas Yet to come was very tall. It was covered with a black garment. It did not speak to Scrooge.

4. Describe the visit to Bob Cratchit's home that Scrooge and The Spirit of Christmas Present made.
   They visited the home of Scrooge's clerk, Bob Cratchit. The Cratchit family members were celebrating, even though they didn't have much material wealth. Tiny Tim was the Cratchits' youngest son. He was sickly and lame. Scrooge wanted to know if Tiny Tim would live or die. The Ghost replied that if things did not change in the future, Tiny Tim would die. Bob Cratchit offered a toast to Scrooge, calling him "The Founder of the Feast." Mrs. Cratchit did not want to drink to his health, saying he was odious and stingy. Bob asked her to do so in the spirit of Christmas, and she did. The children also drank a toast, but did not enjoy it. Tiny Tim said, "God bless us, everyone."

5. The Ghost of Christmas Yet To Come took Scrooge to the city. Describe what they saw in the city. Do not include the visit to Bob Cratchit's house.
   The Spirit took Scrooge to the city. He saw a group of businessmen. They were discussing another businessman's (Old Scratch) death and what he had done with his money. They also wondered who would go to his funeral, since none of them liked him and he had no friends.
   Then the Spirit took Scrooge to an obscure part of town. They saw two men and two women; an old man (Joe), an undertaker's assistant, a charwoman, and a laundress (Mrs. Dilber). They all had bundles that they had taken from the dead man Scrooge had seen earlier. He reacted with horror and disgust. He realized it might be his own unhappy end.
   Next they went to the dead man's home. Scrooge saw the body covered with a cloth. He didn't see the face. He wondered what the man's thoughts would be if he were alive. He thought that avarice and hard dealing had caused an early death.
   Last, the Ghost took Scrooge to the graveyard. he read the name on the tombstone and saw that it was his.

III. Fill-In-The-Blank
1. Ebenezer Scrooge didn't like to celebrate **Christmas.**
2. When his nephew invited him to **Christmas dinner** he refused.
3. Ebenezer didn't want to give his clerk a **whole day off with pay for Christmas**.
4. Scrooge's dead business partner, **Jacob Marley**, appeared to him and told him he needed to change.
5. The Spirit of Christmas **Past** took Scrooge to see his boyhood home and school.
6. The Spirit of Christmas Present took Scrooge to see people who were **happily celebrating Christmas**.
7. The Spirit of Christmas **Present** told Scrooge that if things did not change in the future, his clerk's lame son, Tiny Tim, might die.
8. The Spirit of Christmas **Yet To Come** showed Scrooge three people in a dirty shop.
9. These people had **taken things that belonged to the dead man**.
10. Scrooge was a changed man when he woke up on Christmas day. One of the new and different things he did was **send a turkey to the Cratchit family, have dinner with his nephew, give Bob Cratchit a raise, buy another coal scuttle, become like a second father to Tiny Tim.** (Name any one of the things he did.)

V. Vocbulary Part 1 Choose ten of the vocabulary words to dictate for this section of the test.

Vocabulary Part 2

J	1.	alteration	A.	very bad; offensive
I	2.	blithe	B.	humorous; merry
D	3.	capacious	C.	sadness; depression; gloom
F	4.	disdaining	D.	spacious; large
A	5.	execrable	E.	being everywhere
B	6.	facetious	F.	treating with scorn or contempt
H	7.	inexorable	G.	repaid
C	8.	melancholy	H.	relentless; unyielding
G	9.	recompensed	I.	joyous; happy
E	10.	ubiquitous	J.	change

ADVANCED SHORT ANSWER UNIT TEST *A Christmas Carol*

I. <u>Matching/ Identify</u>

_____ 1. "Bah! Humbug!"   A. Scrooge's reply to his nephew's dinner invitation
_____ 2. Ignorance   B. Tiny Tim's toast
_____ 3. "Good Afternoon!"   C. businessmen's nickname for the dead man
_____ 4. Want   D. Scrooge's response to "Merry Christmas."
_____ 5. Bob Cratchit   E. took the dead Scrooge's sheets and towels
_____ 6. "God bless us, everyone." F. written on the boy's face
_____ 7. Doom   G. the girl under the Spirit's robe
_____ 8. Mrs. Dilber   H. Scrooge's sister
_____ 9. Old Scratch   I. the boy under the Spirit's robe
_____ 10. Fan   J. Scrooge's clerk

II. <u>Short Answer</u>

1. How did Scrooge change over the course of the novel?

2. What are the main themes in the novel? Briefly discuss each.

Advanced Short Answer Unit Test *A Christmas Carol*

3. What was the symbolism of Marley's chains?

4. Describe each of the Spirits and tell where they took Scrooge.

5. What is the setting of the novel? From what point of view is the story told? How did these affect your understanding and enjoyment of the novel?

Advanced Short Answer Unit Test *A Christmas Carol*

III. Quotations Discuss the significance of the following quotations.

1. "I wish to be left alone. Since you ask me what I wish, gentlemen, that is my answer. I don't make merry myself at Christmas, and I can't afford to make idle people merry. I help to support the establishments I have mentioned; they cost enough: and those who are badly off must go there."

2. "Or would you know the weight and length of the strong coil you bear yourself? It was full and heavy and as long as this, seven Christmas Eves ago. You have labored on it, since. It is a ponderous chain!"

3. "It isn't that, Spirit. He has the power to render us happy or unhappy; to make our service light or burdensome; a pleasure or a toil. Say that his power lies in words and looks; in things so slight and insignificant that it is impossible to add and count 'em up; what then? The happiness he gives, is quite as great as if it cost a fortune."

Advanced Short Answer Unit Test *A Christmas Carol*

4. "God bless us every one!"

5. "Men's courses will foreshadow certain ends, to which, if persevered in, they must lead. But if the courses be departed from, the ends will change. Say it is thus with what you show me!"

Advanced Short Answer Unit Test *A Christmas Carol*

IV. Vocabulary

Listen to the words and write them down. After you have written down all of the words, write a paragraph in which you use all of the words. The paragraph must in some way relate to *A Christmas Carol*.

1. _____ 6. _____
2. _____ 7. _____
3. _____ 8. _____
4. _____ 9. _____
5. _____ 10. _____

_____
_____
_____
_____
_____
_____
_____
_____
_____
_____
_____
_____

MULTIPLE CHOICE UNIT TEST 1 *A Christmas Carol*

I. <u>Matching/ Identify</u>

____ 1. Bob Cratchit	A.	showed people toasting Scrooge's health
____ 2. Spirit of Christmas Past	B.	had the power to make others happy or unhappy
____ 3. Spirit of Christmas Present	C.	invited Scrooge to Christmas dinner
____ 4. Christmas Yet to Come	D.	might die in future if present didn't change
____ 5. Tiny Tim	E.	clerk and family man
____ 6. nephew	F.	covetous old sinner
____ 7. Jacob Marley	G.	thought Scrooge loved money more than her
____ 8. Ebenezer Scrooge	H.	came to aid Scrooge's welfare and reclamation
____ 9. Fezziwig	I.	wore the chains he forged in life
____ 10. Belle	J.	showed scene of a dead man who was not mourned

II. <u>Multiple Choice</u>

1. In Stave 1, who visited Scrooge at his warehouse, and what did he want? What was Scrooge's reply?
    A. Scrooge's younger brother came to ask for a job, because he had lost his. Scrooge refused. He said his brother was lazy and should take care of himself.
    B. Scrooge's nephew came to wish him a merry Christmas and invite him for Christmas dinner. He replied only "Good Afternoon" when the nephew invited Scrooge to dinner.
    C. Scrooge's former employer made a social visit. Scrooge bragged about his wealth. The man asked to borrow money and Scrooge refused.
    D. A beggar came asking for a place to spend the night. Scrooge said he could stay if he paid for the space. The beggar went away.

2. True or False: Marley's ghost appeared to Scrooge on Christmas Eve night. It told Scrooge he was doomed to travel the world forever and look at all of the kindness and happiness he had missed. It also said Scrooge was headed on the same path, but still had a chance to redeem himself.
    A. True
    B. False

3. Which of the following sentences does **not** describe the first Spirit?
    A. It was like a child and an old man at the same time.
    B. It had long white hair and a face without wrinkles.
    C. The spirit wore a white tunic trimmed with summer flowers.
    D. There were jets of light coming from its hands.

Multiple Choice Unit Test 1 *A Christmas Carol*

4. Which of the following sentences describes the first scene Scrooge and the Spirit of Christmas Past visited?
   A. It was the young boy who had been singing under Scrooge's window the night before.
   B. They saw Scrooge's parents soon after he had been born.
   C. They saw the city without any poverty.
   D. It was Scrooge's boyhood home and school. They saw Scrooge as a young boy, reading.

5. What was the second place Scrooge visited with the Ghost of Christmas Past?
   A. They visited the graveyard where Scrooge's parents were buried.
   B. They visited Scrooge's nephew.
   C. They visited Scrooge's former master in his warehouse.
   D. They visited the home of Scrooge's clerk, Bob Cratchit.

6. Someone Scrooge saw thought he was a "comical old fellow." He said he felt sorry for Scrooge, that he was the one who really suffered for his own ill whims. Others said they had no patience with him. Who were these people?
   A. The businessmen Scrooge knew said these things.
   B. The first two Spirits said these things.
   C. Scrooge's nephew and nieces said these things.
   D. Scrooge's sister and brother said these things.

7. Who were the two children the Ghost had under its robe?
   A. They were boy twins of Jealousy and Hatred.
   B. The girl was Generosity and the boy was Compassion.
   C. They were both girls. One was Good and the other was Evil.
   D. The boy was Ignorance, and the girl was Want.

8. True or False: Scrooge feared the Ghost of Christmas Yet To Come.
   A. True
   B. False

9. What did Scrooge think about when he saw the dead man?
   A. He wondered if the man knew that no one was sorry he died.
   B. He wondered if the man went to Heaven.
   C. He thought about his own death and vowed to make better preparations in the morning.
   D. He thought that avarice and hard dealing had caused an early death.

Multiple Choice Unit Test 1 *A Christmas Carol*

10. True or False: The Ghost of Jacob Marley visited Scrooge every year to make sure he kept his promises.
    A. True
    B. False

Multiple Choice Unit Test 1 *A Christmas Carol*

III. <u>Quotations</u> Write the letter for the speaker of each quotation on the answer sheet.

A. Scrooge
B. Marley's Ghost
C. Bob Cratchit
D. Tiny Tim
E. Spirit of Christmas Past
F. Spirit of Christmas Present
G. Belle
H. Mrs. Dilber
I. Nephew

1. "It's not my business. It's enough for a man to understand his own business, and not to interfere with other people's. Mine occupies me constantly. Good afternoon, gentlemen!"

2. "I wear the chain I forged in life. I made it link by link, and yard by yard; I girded it on of my own free will, and of my own free will I wore it. Is its pattern strange to you?"

3. "What! Would you so soon put out, with worldly hands, the light I give? Is it not enough that you are one of those whose passions made this cap, and force me through whole trains of years to wear it low upon my brow!"

4. "Home, little Fan?"

5. "You fear the world too much. All your other hopes have merged into the hope of being beyond the chance of its sordid reproach. I have seen your nobler aspirations fall off one by one, until the master-passion, Gain, engrosses you. Have I not?"

6. "There are some upon this earth of yours, who lay claim to know us, and who do their deeds of passion, pride, ill-will, hatred, envy, bigotry, and selfishness in our name, who are as strange to us and all our kith and kin, as if they had never lived. Remember that, and charge their doings on themselves, not us."

7. "As good as gold and better. Somehow he gets thoughtful sitting by himself so much, and thinks the strangest things you ever heard. He told me, coming home, that he hoped the people saw him in the church, because he was a cripple, and it might be pleasant to them to remember upon Christmas Day, who made lame beggars walk and blind men see."

8. "God bless us every one!"

9. "If he wanted to keep 'em after he was dead, a wicked old screw, why wasn't he natural in his lifetime? If he had been, he'd have had somebody to look after him when he was struck with Death, instead of lying gasping out his last there, alone by himself."

10. "Heartily sorry for your good wife. If I can be of any service to you in any way. . . that's where I live. Pray come to me."

IV. <u>Vocabulary Part 1</u> Directions: Write the letter of the matching definition on the blank line.

___ 1.	morose	A.	reclining; lying down
___ 2.	kindred	B.	enormously; hugely
___ 3.	agitated	C.	being courteous with a superior air
___ 4.	recumbent	D.	ill-humored; sullen
___ 5.	supplication	E.	practical rules guiding conduct
___ 6.	condescension	F.	related; belonging to the same family
___ 7.	sordid	G.	asking for humbly or earnestly; praying
___ 8.	prodigiously	H.	meddlesome; self-important
___ 9.	officious	I.	stirred up; disturbed
___ 10.	precepts	J.	filthy; vile

<u>Vocabulary Part 2</u>

Directions: Place the letter of the matching word from the second row on the blank line in front of the definition in the first row.

___ 1. **spacious; large**
   A. capacious   B. morose   C. recumbent   D. sordid

___ 2. **threatening**
   A. resolute   B. fettered   C. inexorable   D. ominous

___ 3. **hateful**
   A. agitated   B. odious   C. facetious   D. portly

___ 4. **going on foot; walking**
   A. illustrious   B. disdaining   C. pedestrian   D. recumbent

___ 5. **sadness; depression; gloom**
   A. destitute   B. melancholy   C. benevolence   D. obscure

___ 6. **angry; furious**
   A. livid   B. infamous   C. sordid   D. inexorable

___ 7. **opponent; enemy**
   A. adversary   B. alteration   C. kindred   D. pedestrian

___ 8. **comfort; compassion**
   A. covetous   B. susceptible   C. extravagance   D. consolation

___ 9. **pretend**
   A. feign   B. livid   C. blithe   D. odious

___ 10. **very bad; offensive**
   A. ubiquitous   B. facetious   C. execrable   D. infamous

MULTIPLE CHOICE UNIT TEST 2 *A Christmas Carol*

I. <u>Matching/ Identify</u>

____ 1. "Bah! Humbug!"   A. Scrooge's reply to his nephew's dinner invitation
____ 2. Ignorance   B. Tiny Tim's toast
____ 3. "Good Afternoon!"   C. businessmen's nickname for the dead man
____ 4. Want   D. Scrooge's response to "Merry Christmas."
____ 5. Bob Cratchit   E. took the dead Scrooge's sheets and towels
____ 6. "God bless us, everyone."   F. written on the boy's face
____ 7. Doom   G. the girl under the Spirit's robe
____ 8. Mrs. Dilber   H. Scrooge's sister
____ 9. Old Scratch   I. the boy under the Spirit's robe
____ 10. Fan   J. Scrooge's clerk

II. <u>Multiple Choice</u>

1. What did the other men who came to the warehouse want? What was Scrooge's reply to them?
   A. They wanted jobs. Scrooge said he would hire them and fire his clerk if they would agree to each work for half of the clerk's salary.
   B. They wanted Scrooge to give money to renovate the church. He told them he did not go to church and would not help to repair it.
   C. They asked for a donation for the poor and destitute. Scrooge replied that he did not make merry, and could not afford to help idle people make merry.
   D. Scrooge was the only businessman who kept his warehouse open on Christmas Day. They tried to persuade him to close, but he refused.

2. True or False: Marley's ghost appeared. He told Scrooge he was doomed to travel the world forever and look at all of the kindness and happiness he had missed. He also said Scrooge was headed on the same path, but still had a chance to redeem himself.
   A. True
   B. False

3. Which of the following sentences does **not** describe the first Spirit?
   A. It was like a child and an old man at the same time.
   B. It had long white hair and a face without wrinkles.
   C. The spirit wore a white tunic trimmed with summer flowers.
   D. There were jets of light coming from its hands.

4. What did Scrooge say to the Ghost about the scene with Fezziwig?
   A. Scrooge said Fezziwig was crazy to spend his money that way.
   B. Scrooge said he never liked the way Fezziwig ran his business, so he did everything the opposite of what he had learned there.
   C. Scrooge said that Fezziwig had the power to make the others happy or unhappy. Scrooge said he wished he could talk to his clerk then.
   D. Scrooge said the things he saw had never really happened. He accused the Spirit of making them up.

5. True or False: Scrooge broke off his engagement to Belle because he wanted to keep all of his money for himself.
   A. True
   B. False

6. Scrooge wanted to know if Tiny Tim would live or die. What was the Spirit's reply?
   A. The Ghost replied that if things did not change in the future, Tiny Tim would die.
   B. The Ghost said it did not know. The next Spirit would give the answer.
   C. The Ghost said there was no hope for Tiny Tim. He would die within a week.
   D. The Ghost said if Scrooge prayed for a miracle, Tiny Tim might live.

7. True or False: When Scrooge asked: "Have they no refuge or resource?" the Spirit replied with Scrooge's own early response: "Are there no prisons? Are there no workhouses?"
   A. True
   B. False

8. How did Scrooge discover who the dead man was?
   A. He heard the undertaker talking about who would pay the funeral bill.
   B. He saw the newspaper headline that said he had died.
   C. The Spirit told him.
   D. Scrooge read his name on the head stone at the graveyard.

9. What did Scrooge tell the Ghost he would do?
   A. He said he would celebrate all holidays except his birthday.
   B. He said he would pray to the three Spirits every day for guidance.
   C. He promised to honor Christmas and keep it all year.
   D. He said he would give away all of his money and live in poverty himself.

Multiple Choice Unit Test 2 *A Christmas Carol*

10. Which of the following did **not** happened at Scrooge's office the morning after Christmas?
    A. Scrooge said he would give Bob Cratchit a raise.
    B. Scrooge also offered to help the family.
    C. Scrooge offered a job to Peter Cratchit.
    D. Scrooge told Bob to buy another coal scuttle.

Multiple Choice Unit Test 2 *A Christmas Carol*

III. <u>Quotations</u> Directions: Write the letter for the speaker of each quotation on the answer sheet.

A. Scrooge	B. Marley's Ghost	C. Bob Cratchit
D. Tiny Tim	E. Spirit of Christmas Past	F. Spirit of Christmas Present
G. Belle	H. Mrs. Dilber	I. Nephew

1. "Home, little Fan?"

2. "I wear the chain I forged in life. I made it link by link, and yard by yard; I girded it on of my own free will, and of my own free will I wore it. Is its pattern strange to you?"

3. "What! Would you so soon put out, with worldly hands, the light I give? Is it not enough that you are one of those whose passions made this cap, and force me through whole trains of years to wear it low upon my brow!"

4. "There are some upon this earth of yours, who lay claim to know us, and who do their deeds of passion, pride, ill-will, hatred, envy, bigotry, and selfishness in our name, who are as strange to us and all our kith and kin, as if they had never lived. Remember that, and charge their doings on themselves, not us."

5. "You fear the world too much. All your other hopes have merged into the hope of being beyond the chance of its sordid reproach. I have seen your nobler aspirations fall off one by one, until the master-passion, Gain, engrosses you. Have I not?"

6. "Heartily sorry for your good wife. If I can be of any service to you in any way. . . that's where I live. Pray come to me."

7. "God bless us every one!"

8. "As good as gold and better. Somehow he gets thoughtful sitting by himself so much, and thinks the strangest things you ever heard. He told me, coming home, that he hoped the people saw him in the church, because he was a cripple, and it might be pleasant to them to remember upon Christmas Day, who made lame beggars walk and blind men see."

9. "If he wanted to keep 'em after he was dead, a wicked old screw, why wasn't he natural in his lifetime? If he had been, he'd have had somebody to look after him when he was struck with Death, instead of lying gasping out his last there, alone by himself."

10. "It's not my business. It's enough for a man to understand his own business, and not to interfere with other people's. Mine occupies me constantly. Good afternoon, gentlemen!"

Multiple Choice Unit Test 2 *A Christmas Carol*

IV. Vocabulary Part 1 Directions: Place the letter of the matching definition on the blank line.

____	1. alteration	A.	very bad; offensive
____	2. blithe	B.	humorous; merry
____	3. capacious	C.	sadness; depression; gloom
____	4. disdaining	D.	spacious; large
____	5. execrable	E.	being everywhere
____	6. facetious	F.	treating with scorn or contempt
____	7. inexorable	G.	repaid
____	8. melancholy	H.	relentless; unyielding
____	9. recompensed	I.	joyous; happy
____	10. ubiquitous	J.	change

Vocabulary Part 2 Directions: Place the letter of the matching word from the second row on the blank line in front of the definition in the first row.

____ 1. **softens in attitude or temper**
   A. relents   B. consolation   C. detestation   D. benevolence

____ 2. **pleads on another's behalf**
   A. covetous   B. capacious   C. intercedes   D. encompass

____ 3. **glorious; brilliant**
   A. prodigiously   B. facetious   C. inexorable   D. illustrious

____ 4. **hateful**
   A. blithe   B. livid   C. odious   D. cordially

____ 5. **complete agreement**
   A. resolute   B. unanimity   C. destitute   D. inexorable

____ 6. **determined**
   A. recompensed   B. relents   C. dispelled   D. resolute

____ 7. **to surround**
   A. remonstrated   B. officious   C. obscure   D. encompass

____ 8. **poor; penniless**
   A. disdaining   B. destitute   C. blithe   D. illustrious

____ 9. **stout; fat**
   A. ubiquitous   B. portly   C. agitated   D. destitute

____ 10. **intense dislike; aversion**
   A. agitated   B. supplication   C. detestation   D. adversary

ANSWER SHEET   MULTIPLE CHOICE UNIT TESTS *A Christmas Carol*

<u>I. Matching</u>

1. _____
2. _____
3. _____
4. _____
5. _____
6. _____
7. _____
8. _____
9. _____
10. _____

<u>II. Multiple Choice</u>

1. (A) (B) (C) (D)
2. (A) (B) (C) (D)
3. (A) (B) (C) (D)
4. (A) (B) (C) (D)
5. (A) (B) (C) (D)
6. (A) (B) (C) (D)
7. (A) (B) (C) (D)
8. (A) (B) (C) (D)
9. (A) (B) (C) (D)
10. (A) (B) (C) (D)

<u>III. Quotations</u>

1. _____
2. _____
3. _____
4. _____
5. _____
6. _____
7. _____
8. _____
9. _____
10. _____

<u>IV. Vocabulary</u>

1. _____
2. _____
3. _____
4. _____
5. _____
6. _____
7. _____
8. _____
9. _____
10. _____

<u>Part 2</u>

1. _____
2. _____
3. _____
4. _____
5. _____
6. _____
7. _____
8. _____
9. _____
10. _____

ANSWER SHEET KEY Multiple Choice Unit Test 1 *A Christmas Carol*

I. Matching	III. Quotations	IV. Vocabulary
1. E	1. A	1. D
2. H	2. B	2. F
3. A	3. E	3. I
4. J	4. A	4. A
5. D	5. G	5. G
6. C	6. F	6. C
7. I	7. C	7. J
8. F	8. D	8. B
9. B	9. H	9. H
10. G	10. I	10. E

II. Multiple Choice

1. (A) ( ) (C) (D)
2. ( ) (B) (C) (D)
3. (A) (B) (C) ( )
4. (A) (B) (C) ( )
5. (A) (B) ( ) (D)
6. (A) (B) ( ) (D)
7. (A) (B) (C) ( )
8. ( ) (B) (C) (D)
9. (A) (B) (C) ( )
10. (A) ( ) (C) (D)

Part 2

1. A
2. D
3. B
4. C
5. B
6. A
7. A
8. D
9. A
10. C

ANSWER SHEET KEY Multiple Choice Unit Test 2 *A Christmas Carol*

I. Matching	III. Quotations	IV. Vocabulary
1. D	1. A	1. J
2. I	2. B	2. I
3. A	3. E	3. D
4. G	4. F	4. F
5. J	5. G	5. A
6. B	6. I	6. B
7. F	7. D	7. H
8. E	8. C	8. C
9. C	9. H	9. G
10. H	10. A	10. E

II. Multiple Choice
1. (A) (B) ( ) (D)
2. ( ) (B) (C) (D)
3. (A) (B) (C) ( )
4. (A) (B) ( ) (D)
5. (A) ( ) (C) (D)
6. ( ) (B) (C) (D)
7. ( ) (B) (C) (D)
8. (A) (B) (C) ( )
9. (A) (B) ( ) (D)
10. (A) B) ( ) (D)

Part 2
1. A
2. C
3. D
4. C
5. B
6. D
7. D
8. B
9. B
10. C

UNIT RESOURCES

BULLETIN BOARD IDEAS

1. Save one corner of the board for the best of students' *A Christmas Carol* writing assignments. You may want to use background maps of Europe to represent the setting of the novel.

2. Take one of the word search puzzles from the extra activities packet and with a marker copy it over in a large size on the bulletin board. Write the clue words to find to one side. Invite students prior to and after class to find the words and circle them on the bulletin board.

3. Have students find or draw pictures that they think resemble the people in the book.

4. Invite students to help make an interactive bulletin board quiz. Give each student a half-sheet of paper (about 4"x5') folded in half so that it can open. On the outside flap, have each student write a description of one of the characters in the text. On the inside, they will write the name of the character. You can staple or tack these papers to the bulletin board so that the students can read the descriptions and lift the flaps to find the answers.

5. Collect pictures of London, especially in the late 1800s.

6. Make a display of pictures of book jackets and artwork from the various editions of *A Christmas Carol*. You may want to include pictures from the movies based on the book.

7. Display articles about Charles Dickens and/or *A Christmas Carol*.

8. Have students design postcards depicting the settings of the book.

9. Display a large map of London.

10. Display reviews of Dickens's works.

EXTRA ACTIVITIES *A Christmas Carol*

One of the difficulties in teaching a novel is that all students don't read at the same speed. One student who likes to read may take the book home and finish it in a day or two. Sometimes a few students finish the in-class assignments early. The problem, then, is finding suitable extra activities for students.

One thing that helps is to keep a little library in the classroom. For this unit on *A Christmas Carol* you might check out from the school or public library other books by Charles Dickens. There are also many other holiday-related novels that students would enjoy reading. Several journals have critiques of Dickens's works. Some of the students may enjoy reading these and responding either in writing or in discussion groups.

Your students who have reading difficulties, or speak English as a second language may benefit from listening to all or part of the book on tape. Ask parents, other volunteers, or fluent readers in your class to make a tape.

Other things you may keep on hand are word search puzzles. Several puzzles relating directly to *A Christmas Carol* are included in the unit. Feel free to duplicate them.

Some students may like to draw. You might devise a contest or allow some extra-credit grade for students who draw characters or scenes from *A Christmas Carol.* Note, too, that if the students do not want to keep their drawings you may pick up some extra bulletin board materials this way. If you have a contest and you supply the prize. You could, possibly, make the drawing itself a non-refundable entry fee.

Have maps, a globe, and travel brochures on hand for easy reference. Travel agencies and automobile clubs are good sources for these materials.

The pages which follow contain games, puzzles, and worksheets. The keys, when appropriate, immediately follow the puzzle or worksheet. There are two main groups of activities: one group for the unit; that is, generally relating to the text, and another group of activities related strictly to the vocabulary for *A Christmas Carol.*

Directions for the games, puzzles, and worksheets are self-explanatory. The object here is to provide you with extra materials you may use in any way you choose.

MORE ACTIVITIES *A Christmas Carol*

1. Pick one of the scenes for students to dramatize. Encourage students to write dialog for the characters. (Perhaps you could assign various stories to different groups of students so more than one story could be acted and more students could participate.)

2. Have students design a book cover (front and back and inside flaps) for *A Christmas Carol.*

3. Have students design a bulletin board (ready to be put up; not just sketched) for *A Christmas Carol.*

4. Invite a story teller to tell one or more stories related to *A Christmas Carol* to the class.

5. Use some of the related topics (noted earlier for an in-class library) as topics for research, reports, or written papers, or as topics for guest speakers.

6. Help students design and produce a talk show. Choose one of the story incidents as the topic. The host will interview the various characters. (Students should make up the questions they want the host to ask the characters.)

7. Have students work in pairs to create an interview with one of the characters. One student should be the interviewer and the other should be the interviewee. Students can work together to compose questions for the interviewer to ask. Each pair of students could present their interview to the class.

8. Invite students who have read other books by Charles Dickens to present booktalks to the class.

9. Make book markers with a favorite scene from the book.

10. Invite students who have read a biography of Charles Dickens to tell the class about his life.

11. Write a radio or television commercial to advertise the book.

12. Design a poster to advertise the book.

13. Invite someone who has lived in or visited London to speak to the class.

14. Have students hold small group discussions related to topics in the book. Assign a recorder and a speaker for each group. Have the speaker from each group make a report to the class.

15. Have students work in small groups to write a sequel telling what happened to Scrooge.

16. Make a mobile showing the main characters, setting, and a few events.

17. Make a comic book version of the book to share with younger readers.

18. Make a collage based on scenes from the book.

19. Write a different ending to the story.

20. Make puppets and write a puppet show based on the book.

UNIT WORD SEARCH

All the words in this list are associated with *A Christmas Carol*. The words are placed backwards, forward, diagonally, up and down. The words used in the puzzle are listed below.

```
L N P C M Y E X Y R C X Q Z N R J O R M E E Y O T V M T R L
F O K F G R Q E C M N I W W E C X M B N Q S J R E N A A G K
K X N V M O T M A L F V F B P Y T B D D A F A M I L R W P Q
P X G D X T R I J D Z M J K H A E M Z U A Q Z H J T L D K B
O C U T O O K T A E U A S K E M S C M E H H V K O Y E E O M
B A U C Q N K Y P P T U V B W Y E N N G U B M U H D Y B B Z
T F O C I R W N T Z Z V Q H R S W Q V A F G N I W X C Q Q V
M M S M O O D I D F X S S C T V F G H C R H D F F R T E D Z
E W U V W H X T O S E H C L G I Z E B B Q O H I A E X L Z D
C W R V P K C U O B C Z P X D A L S L J K T N T N L D Y Q Y
T H C A F L D M R H W P Z C Q E E N P Y K K C G K D F Y Q J
V N A D J S B W K V O S F I V M P E Z X Z H P A I R H U S Q
I P E I X Y Z M N F M J X X W O A K Y M I O G A G O R C H J
Z R W S N J T T O L N H U H P I M C B T S M T L Y P R M V O
D U O S E S L S C P N Z E N L F G I D E Z D K M S O M S S G
U Q T F W R Z A K Z B D P N P R Q D V F F P I Q O F U K W S
Q X K N A N P P E B S V V R R I L H E N P N W G A Q W D L Z
W Z O B N Z U G R J S H Z Z Y C E I L W J F E N Y B B W V F
P M R M T G R A V E S T O N E O H X Z P B U W T S X C F P L
```

SCROOGE	FEZZIWIG	C HAINS
MARLEY	TINY TIM	DOOM
NEPHEW	BOB CRATCHIT	FAN
HUMBUG	WANT	DOOR KNOCKER
PAST	IGNORANCE	GRAVE STONE
PRESENT	LONDON	BELLE
YET TO COME	DICKENS	

CROSSWORD *Christmas Carol*

CROSSWORD CLUES *Christmas Carol*

ACROSS
1 Scrooge's place of business
3 Scrooge's first name
5 Setting of novel
7 Scrooge sent it to the Cratchit home
9 Garment color of Spirit of Christmas Yet To Come
12 Worn by first Spirit: extinguisher ___
13 Last spirit showed Scrooge his name on a ___ stone
15 Cratchit's older son, looking for a job
17 Written on the boy's brow
19 Laundress who took Scrooge's things
20 Cratchit's lame youngest son: Tiny ___
21 Nickname for the dead businessman: Old ___
23 Scrooge's sister
26 Said Tiny Tim might die
31 Took Scrooge's seal, pencil case, sleeve-buttons, and brooch
33 Scrooge's former fiancee
34 The boy under the spirit's robe
35 Scrooge did not miss it

DOWN
1 The girl under the spirit's robe
2 Scrooge told Bob to buy a new coal ___
3 When Marley appeared: Christmas ___
4 What the first spirit came for
5 Mrs. Dilber's job
6 Invited Scrooge to Christmas dinner
8 It turned into Marley's face
10 Old man looking at Scrooge's things
11 Scrooge's former master
13 Robe color of Spirit of Christmas Present
14 Marley was wearing the ones he forged in life
14 White hair; face without wrinkles
16 Where Scrooge ate
18 Cratchit's daughter
22 Pretended to be blind during the game
23 Scrooge's nephew
24 Scrooge's clerk Bob
25 Dead partner
27 Covetous old sinner
28 Author
29 Scrooge's expression
30 Tunic color of the Spirit of Christmas Past
32 Marley's first name

CROSSWORD ANSWER KEY *Christmas Carol*

MATCHING QUIZ/WORKSHEET 1 - CHRISTMAS CAROL

___ 1. HUMBUG　　　　　A. The girl under the spirit's robe

___ 2. FAN　　　　　　　B. Scrooge told Bob to buy a new coal ___

___ 3. FRED　　　　　　C. Pretended to be blind during the game

___ 4. EVE　　　　　　　D. Tunic color of the Spirit of Christmas Past

___ 5. PETER　　　　　　E. Dead partner

___ 6. UNDERTAKER　　　F. Scrooge's expression

___ 7. LAUNDRESS　　　　G. Mrs. Dilber's job

___ 8. TIM　　　　　　　H. Cratchit's older son, looking for a job

___ 9. PRESENT　　　　　I. Cratchit's daughter

___10. WANT　　　　　　J. Old man looking at Scrooge's things

___11. BELLE　　　　　　K. Nickname for the dead businessman: Old ___

___12. SCRATCH　　　　　L. Setting of novel

___13. TOPPER　　　　　M. Cratchit's lame youngest son: Tiny ___

___14. SCUTTLE　　　　　N. Scrooge's nephew

___15. DOOM　　　　　　O. Took Scrooge's seal, pencil case, sleeve-buttons, and brooch

___16. MARLEY　　　　　P. Scrooge's sister

___17. EBENEZER　　　　Q. When Marley appeared: Christmas ___

___18. INVITATION　　　R. White hair; face without wrinkles

___19. LONDON　　　　　S. Where Scrooge ate

___20. CHAINS　　　　　T. Marley was wearing the ones he forged in life

___21. PAST　　　　　　U. Good afternoon was Scrooge's reply to his nephew's ___

___22. JOE　　　　　　　V. Written on the boy's brow

___23. TAVERN　　　　　W. Scrooge's first name

___24. WHITE　　　　　　X. Said Tiny Tim might die

___25. MARTHA　　　　　Y. Scrooge's former fiancee

KEY: MATCHING QUIZ/WORKSHEET 1 - CHRISTMAS CAROL

F - 1. HUMBUG   A. The girl under the spirit's robe
P - 2. FAN   B. Scrooge told Bob to buy a new coal ___
N - 3. FRED   C. Pretended to be blind during the game
Q - 4. EVE   D. Tunic color of the Spirit of Christmas Past
H - 5. PETER   E. Dead partner
O - 6. UNDERTAKER   F. Scrooge's expression
G - 7. LAUNDRESS   G. Mrs. Dilber's job
M - 8. TIM   H. Cratchit's older son, looking for a job
X - 9. PRESENT   I. Cratchit's daughter
A -10. WANT   J. Old man looking at Scrooge's things
Y -11. BELLE   K. Nickname for the dead businessman: Old ___
K -12. SCRATCH   L. Setting of novel
C -13. TOPPER   M. Cratchit's lame youngest son: Tiny ___
B -14. SCUTTLE   N. Scrooge's nephew
V -15. DOOM   O. Took Scrooge's seal, pencil case, sleeve-buttons, and brooch
E -16. MARLEY   P. Scrooge's sister
W 17. EBENEZER   Q. When Marley appeared: Christmas ___
U -18. INVITATION   R. White hair; face without wrinkles
L -19. LONDON   S. Where Scrooge ate
T -20. CHAINS   T. Marley was wearing the ones he forged in life
R -21. PAST   U. Good afternoon was Scrooge's reply to his nephew's ___
J -22. JOE   V. Written on the boy's brow
S -23. TAVERN   W. Scrooge's first name
D -24. WHITE   X. Said Tiny Tim might die
I -25. MARTHA   Y. Scrooge's former fiancee

MATCHING QUIZ/WORKSHEET 2 - CHRISTMAS CAROL

___ 1. SCROOGE   A. Scrooge's clerk Bob
___ 2. BLACK   B. Nickname for the dead businessman: Old ___
___ 3. FAN   C. What first spirit came for
___ 4. PRESENT   D. Author
___ 5. TOPPER   E. Old man looking at Scrooge's things
___ 6. CRATCHIT   F. Scrooge's sister
___ 7. CHAINS   G. Tunic color of the Spirit of Christmas Past
___ 8. TURKEY   H. Where Scrooge ate
___ 9. PETER   I. Setting of novel
___10. GREEN   J. Garment color of Spirit of Christmas Yet To Come
___11. FEZZIWIG   K. Cratchit's older son, looking for a job
___12. JOE   L. Covetous old sinner
___13. EVE   M. Said Tiny Tim might die
___14. RECLAMATION   N. Robe color of Spirit of Christmas Present
___15. DICKENS   O. Scrooge's nephew
___16. MARLEY   P. Scrooge sent it to the Cratchit home
___17. LONDON   Q. Scrooge's former master
___18. SCRATCH   R. Marley was wearing the ones he forged in life
___19. UNDERTAKER   S. Took Scrooge's seal, pencil case, sleeve-buttons, and brooch
___20. MARTHA   T. Cratchit's daughter
___21. TAVERN   U. When Marley appeared: Christmas ___
___22. INVITATION   V. Dead partner
___23. WHITE   W. Last spirit showed Scrooge his name on a ___ stone
___24. GRAVE   X. Good afternoon was Scrooge's reply to his nephew's ___
___25. FRED   Y. Pretended to be blind during the game

KEY: MATCHING QUIZ/WORKSHEET 2 - CHRISTMAS CAROL

L - 1. SCROOGE   A. Scrooge's clerk Bob
J - 2. BLACK   B. Nickname for the dead businessman: Old ___
F - 3. FAN   C. What first spirit came for
M - 4. PRESENT   D. Author
Y - 5. TOPPER   E. Old man looking at Scrooge's things
A - 6. CRATCHIT   F. Scrooge's sister
R - 7. CHAINS   G. Tunic color of the Spirit of Christmas Past
P - 8. TURKEY   H. Where Scrooge ate
K - 9. PETER   I. Setting of novel
N -10. GREEN   J. Garment color of Spirit of Christmas Yet To Come
Q -11. FEZZIWIG   K. Cratchit's older son, looking for a job
E -12. JOE   L. Covetous old sinner
U -13. EVE   M. Said Tiny Tim might die
C -14. RECLAMATION   N. Robe color of Spirit of Christmas Present
D -15. DICKENS   O. Scrooge's nephew
V -16. MARLEY   P. Scrooge sent it to the Cratchit home
I -17. LONDON   Q. Scrooge's former master
B -18. SCRATCH   R. Marley was wearing the ones he forged in life
S -19. UNDERTAKER   S. Took Scrooge's seal, pencil case, sleeve-buttons, and brooch
T -20. MARTHA   T. Cratchit's daughter
H -21. TAVERN   U. When Marley appeared: Christmas ___
X -22. INVITATION   V. Dead partner
G -23. WHITE   W. Last spirit showed Scrooge his name on a ___ stone
W 24. GRAVE   X. Good afternoon was Scrooge's reply to his nephew's ___
O -25. FRED   Y. Pretended to be blind during the game

UNIT SCRAMBLED WORD GAME *A Christmas Carol*

Scrambled	Word	Clue
OGRESOC	SCROOGE	covetous old sinner
RAYLEM	MARLEY	dead partner
GHMBUU	HUMBUG	Scrooge's expression
NHEPWE	NEPHEW	invited Scrooge to Christmas dinner
NIKCESD	DICKENS	author
ZBERNEEE	EBENEZER	Scrooge's first name
ACBOJ	JACOB	Marley's first name
HITMAERCS VES	CHRISTMAS EVE	when Marley appeared
DHICSTMASAYR	CHRISTMAS DAY	Scrooge didn't miss it
CRODOKRNOKE	DOOR KNOCKER	turned into Marley's face
VAERNT	TAVERN	where Scrooge ate
NGOAEOFROTOND	GOOD AFTERNOON	Scrooge's reply to his nephew's invitation
STAP	PAST	white hair, face without wrinkles
NTREESP	PRESENT	said Tiny Tim might die
OETOCMEYTT	YET TO COME	showed Scrooge his tombstone
ANF	FAN	Scrooge's sister
GZEZIWIF	FEZZIWIG	Scrooge's former master
ELEBL	BELLE	Scrooge's former fiancee
MINTYIT	TINY TIM	Cratchit's lame youngest son
BRATTBOCCHI	BOB CRATCHIT	Scrooge's clerk
FERD	FRED	Scrooge's nephew
PPEROT	TOPPER	pretended to be blind during the game
NOAGNCEIR	IGNORANCE	the boy under the Spirit's robe
TAWN	WANT	the girl under the Spirit's robe
DCSCOALTHR	OLD SCRATCH	nickname for the dead businessman
RDILSBEMR	MRS. DILBER	laundress who took Scrooge's things
OJE	JOE	old man who looked at Scrooge's things
OMOD	DOOM	written on the boy's brow
BCKAL	BLACK	Christmas Yet to Come's garment color
MACWOHANR	CHARWOMAN	took Scrooge's bed curtains
ANRESSLDU	LAUNDRESS	Mrs. Dilber
NERTKUERDA	UNDERTAKER	seal, pencil case, sleeve-buttons, brooch
ETRPE	PETER	Cratchit's older son, looking for a job
UKEYRT	TURKEY	Scrooge sent it to the Cratchit home
TOLSCUTLAEC	COAL SCUTTLE	Scrooge told Bob to buy a new one
ODONNL	LONDON	setting of novel
AEHOWRUSE	WAREHOUSE	Scrooge's place of business
ATHARM	MARTHA	Cratchit daughter
VRAESTEOGN	GRAVE STONE	last spirit showed Scrooge his name on it

HACNSI	CHAINS	Marley wore the ones he forged in life
TEHWI	WHITE	Tunic color of Spirit of Christmas Past
XTIPENAUISGHECR	EXTINGUISHER CAP	worn by first Spirit
CLRAMAETINO	RECLAMATION	what first Spirit came for
RENEG	GREEN	color of Spirit of Christmas Present's robe

VOCABULARY RESOURCES

VOCABULARY WORD SEARCH *A Christmas Carol*

```
C M V Y M P T F R E T O R W E D U D I V L I H O B E H T I L B X M V
C H L A S T Y W H W P L T O L E E D Q I F K E G F L H F V K D C L Z
M Q B H D X Y N H C P B N J B P O L L Y E V O E O F X M K S I P H P
F J Y S P N P X V Z R H L U A Y B E L I Y C J Y O B I K Y M V U N D
K Z B G Z M V M B V M G C S R P P M H E L K C Q J O V C B S I W F G
N W E U C A S T S S A P M O C N E V U J P J P F B Y G K I N L F Z Y
J B C R K T K A Q U P T Y M E P D P C J N S G Q G U D S S O P J T V
E P K J U E B X L O R N Y N X G W X X R W S I O M O R D A B U E H T
L Z T K P C R U G I O G S D E Q L J Y Y N I A D S X E X P O P S F K
Y S K T O I S T Q R D P P V Y C L G S I O F U P N P E K O Q V B T U
E N V R F A C B K T I H E C C O W A U I F E Y L A N B H R K I D U T
U L J V B C L S O S G E J A U H A V G T T B M F O M O W E W V W X O
A P B P E N R I L U I O Y B Y G A T O Z D O G Y Z Y D O T M M T B R
B L A A A K J A N L O B N T U Z G L B G R E V E R C I U I M E I I P
L A T R R L F L C L U K A J I R E K C S U Z J T U K U Q O N G R W D
X I D E Q O P X Y I S Q T W G M Z B J E P A E J Q R M Y L R G V K H
Y S B Y R D X J X P L Q Z M T Q I I E O L F V J S R R D K E D H T L
I P S Q I A R E M Z Y T H K D D P N G N L B A J T P R A B L I Q R C
Q J A E F R T R N J G I Q V Q J T L A U D R D H B Z H Q Z E D T U F
C B O W M T Y I W I K U Q R A O V N T N R W K J I T E K E N Y F Q Y
F H X G B I Q B O A H G X E U T M H J B U O L K K S E M E T B L N O
H F J D W F K U X N R P E A N C D A G N I N I A D S I D F S Q G J D
```

PRODIGIOUSLY	ENCOMPASS	DISPELLED
DISDAINING	OBSCURE	ILLUSTRIOUS
OFFICIOUS	LOITER	BLITHE
LIVID	RELENTS	UNANIMITY
EXECRABLE	INEXORABLE	ALTERATION

VOCABULARY CROSSWORD *Christmas Carol*

VOCABULARY CROSSWORD CLUES *Christmas Carol*

ACROSS
1 Asking for humbly or earnestly
4 Humorous; merry
7 Practical rules guiding conduct
9 Being everywhere
11 Well-known for bad reasons
13 Protested
17 Hateful
20 Related; belonging to the same family
22 Hang around; linger
25 Glorious; brilliant
26 Joyous; happy
27 Desirous of what someone else has
28 Stout; fat
29 Shackled; chained

DOWN
1 Filthy; vile
2 Relentless; unyielding
3 Pleads on another's behalf
5 Stirred up; disturbed
6 Complete agreement
8 Spirit
10 Generosity; kindness
12 Change
14 Ill-humored; sullen
15 Surround
16 Determined
17 Meddlesome; self-important
18 Very bad; offensive
19 Going on foot; walking
21 Scattered; caused to vanish
22 Angry; furious
23 Softens in attitude or temper
24 Dark; vague; unclear

VOCABULARY CROSSWORD ANSWER KEY *Christmas Carol*

```
S U P P L I C A T I O N . . . F A C E T I O U S
O . . . N . . N . . . . . G . . . . . . N
R . . P R E C E P T S . U B I Q U I T O U S . A
D . . X . S . E . . . E . . T . . . . . . N
I N F A M O U S . R E M O N S T R A T E D . I
D . . L . R . C . O . E . . T . N . R . . M
. . . T . A . N . R . V . . E . C . E . . I
. . . E . B . C . D . O . O D I O U S . . T
. . . R . L . E . E . S . F . M . O . . Y
E . . A . E . S . E . . . F . P . L
X . . T . . P . . . . . N . I . A . U
E . K I N D R E D . . . C . C . S . T
C . . O . I . D . L O I T E R . I . S . E . O
R . . N . S . E . I . . E . O . . . . . . B
A . . . . P . S . V . . . I L L U S T R I O U S
B L I T H E . T . I . . . E . S . . . . . C
L . . . L . R . D . . . N . . C O V E T O U S
E . . . L . I . . . P O R T L Y . . . . . R
. . . . E . A . . . . . . S . F E T T E R E D
. . . . D . N
```

VOCABULARY MATCHING *A Christmas Carol*

Directions: Place the letter of the matching definition on the blank line.

____ 1.	abstinence	A.	relentless; unyielding
____ 2.	alteration	B.	pretend
____ 3.	benevolence	C.	being courteous with a superior air
____ 4.	capacious	D.	protested
____ 5.	condescension	E.	enormously; hugely
____ 6.	cordially	F.	repaid
____ 7.	covetous	G.	spacious; large
____ 8.	disdaining	H.	determined
____ 9.	extravagance	I.	being everywhere
____ 10.	facetious	J.	avaricious; greedy
____ 11.	feign	K.	avoidance
____ 12.	inexorable	L.	impressionable; easily influenced
____ 13.	obscure	M.	humorous; merry
____ 14.	prodigiously	N.	treating with scorn or contempt
____ 15.	recompensed	O.	generosity; kindness
____ 16.	remonstrated	P.	extremely abundant; excessive
____ 17.	resolute	Q.	asking for humbly or earnestly; praying
____ 18.	supplication	R.	dark; vague; unclear
____ 19.	susceptible	S.	change
____ 20.	ubiquitous	T.	graciously; in a friendly way

ANSWER KEY VOCABULARY MATCHING *A Christmas Carol*

Directions: Place the letter of the matching definition on the blank line.

K	1.	abstinence	A.	relentless; unyielding
S	2.	alteration	B.	pretend
O	3.	benevolence	C.	being courteous with a superior air
G	4.	capacious	D.	protested
C	5.	condescension	E.	enormously; hugely
T	6.	cordially	F.	repaid
J	7.	covetous	G.	spacious; large
N	8.	disdaining	H.	determined
P	9.	extravagance	I.	being everywhere
M	10.	facetious	J.	avaricious; greedy
B	11.	feign	K.	avoidance
A	12.	inexorable	L.	impressionable; easily influenced
R	13.	obscure	M.	humorous; merry
E	14.	prodigiously	N.	treating with scorn or contempt
F	15.	recompensed	O.	generosity; kindness
D	16.	remonstrated	P.	extremely abundant; excessive
H	17.	resolute	Q.	asking for humbly or earnestly; praying
Q	18.	supplication	R.	dark; vague; unclear
L	19.	susceptible	S.	change
I	20.	ubiquitous	T.	graciously; in a friendly way

VOCABULARY MULTIPLE CHOICE *A Christmas Carol*

_____ 1. **ill humored; sullen**
A. capacious B. **morose** C. recumbent D. sordid

_____ 2. **threatening**
A. resolute B. fettered C. inexorable D. **ominous**

_____ 3. **stirred up; disturbed**
A. **agitated** B. odious C. facetious D. portly

_____ 4. **going on foot; walking**
A. illustrious B. disdaining C. **pedestrian** D. recumbent

_____ 5. **sadness; depression; gloom**
A. destitute B. **melancholy** C. benevolence D. obscure

_____ 6. **filthy; vile**
A. livid B. infamous C. **sordid** D. inexorable

_____ 7. **opponent; enemy**
A. **adversary** B. alteration C. kindred D. pedestrian

_____ 8. **comfort; compassion**
A. covetous B. susceptible C. extravagance D. **consolation**

_____ 9. **angry; furious**
A. feign B. **livid** C. blithe D. odious

_____ 10. **very bad; offensive**
A. ubiquitous B. facetious C. **execrable** D. infamous

_____ 11. **softens in attitude or temper**
A. **relents** B. consolation C. detestation D. benevolence

_____ 12. **pleads on another's behalf**
A. covetous B. capacious C. **intercedes** D. encompass

_____ 13. **glorious; brilliant**
A. prodigiously B. facetious C. inexorable D. **illustrious**

_____ 14. **joyous; happy**
A. **blithe** B. livid C. odious D. cordially

_____ 15. **complete agreement**
A. resolute B. **unanimity** C. destitute D. inexorable

_____ 16. **repaid**
A. **recompensed** B. relents C. dispelled D. resolute

_____ 17. **to surround**
A. remonstrated B. officious C. obscure D. **encompass**

_____ 18. **poor; penniless**
A. disdaining B. **destitute** C. blithe D. illustrious

_____ 19. **meddlesome; self-important**
A. **officious** B. portly C. agitated D. destitute

_____ 20. **intense dislike; aversion**
A. agitated B. supplication C. **detestation** D. adversary

ANSWER KEY VOCABULARY MULTIPLE CHOICE *A Christmas Carol*

B 1. ill humored; sullen
A. capacious B. **morose** C. recumbent D. sordid

D 2. threatening
A. resolute B. fettered C. inexorable D. **ominous**

A 3. stirred up; disturbed
A. **agitated** B. odious C. facetious D. portly

C 4. going on foot; walking
A. illustrious B. disdaining C. **pedestrian** D. recumbent

B 5. sadness; depression; gloom
A. destitute B. **melancholy** C. benevolence D. obscure

C 6. filthy; vile
A. livid B. infamous C. **sordid** D. inexorable

A 7. opponent; enemy
A. **adversary** B. alteration C. kindred D. pedestrian

D 8. comfort; compassion
A. covetous B. susceptible C. extravagance D. **consolation**

B 9. angry; furious
A. feign B. **livid** C. blithe D. odious

C 10. very bad; offensive
A. ubiquitous B. facetious C. **execrable** D. infamous

A 11. softens in attitude or temper
A. **relents** B. consolation C. detestation D. benevolence

C 12. pleads on another's behalf
A. covetous B. capacious C. **intercedes** D. encompass

D 13. glorious; brilliant
A. prodigiously B. facetious C. inexorable D. **illustrious**

A 14. joyous; happy
A. **blithe** B. livid C. odious D. cordially

B 15. complete agreement
A. resolute B. **unanimity** C. destitute D. inexorable

A 16. repaid
A. **recompensed** B. relents C. dispelled D. resolute

D 17. to surround
A. remonstrated B. officious C. obscure D. **encompass**

B 18. poor; penniless
A. disdaining B. **destitute** C. blithe D. illustrious

A 19. meddlesome; self-important
A. **officious** B. portly C. agitated D. destitute

C 20. intense dislike; aversion
A. agitated B. supplication C. **detestation** D. adversary

VOCABULARY WORD SCRAMBLE *A Christmas Carol*

BANTINCSEE	ABSTINENCE	avoidance
YAVRSADRE	ADVERSARY	opponent; enemy
TGITDAAE	AGITATED	stirred up; disturbed
LEARNOATTI	ALTERATION	change
LEEBVCOENNE	BENEVOLENCE	generosity; kindness
ITHLEB	BLITHE	joyous; happy
OAPAUSCCI	CAPACIOUS	spacious; large
NONCDCEENSIOS	CONDESCENSION	being courteous with a superior air
SONCOOLNTIA	CONSOLATION	comfort; compassion
AOLRCDILY	CORDIALLY	graciously; in a friendly way
CESTOOVU	COVETOUS	avaricious; eagerly desirous of; greedy
DTSUTITEE	DESTITUTE	poor; penniless
TDNEEOTATIS	DETESTATION	intense dislike; aversion
ASDGINIIND	DISDAINING	treating with scorn or contempt
DISPEELDL	DISPELLED	scattered; caused ot vanish
COSMNPASE	ENCOMPASS	to surround
SNSEECE	ESSENCE	spirit
AXEBLREEC	EXECRABLE	very bad; offensive
VAXTAECRAGNE	EXTRAVAGANCE	extremely abundant; excessive
FSCEIOAUT	FACETIOUS	humorous; merry
IGNFE	FEIGN	pretend
TEDTERFE	FETTERED	shackled; chained
LOUISTRUSIL	ILLUSTRIOUS	glorious; brilliant
LEXONRAIBE	INEXORABLE	relentless; unyielding
FOIMNUSA	INFAMOUS	notoriously bad
TSENCEIDER	INTERCEDES	pleads on another's behalf

VOCABULARY WORD SCRAMBLE

IRNDEDK	KINDRED	related; belonging to the same family
AENTTL	LATENT	dormant; hidden
VIIDL	LIVID	angry; furious
TEROIL	LOITER	hang around; linger
OELYANMCHL	MELANCHOLY	sadnesses; depression; gloom
EROOMS	MOROSE	ill-humored; sullen
BOCSREU	OBSCURE	dark; vague; unclear
SIOUOD	ODIOUS	hateful
FIIOUFSCO	OFFICIOUS	meddlesome; self-important
MUIOOSN	OMINOUS	threatening
SPEEDTRAIN	PEDESTRIAN	going on foot; walking
LOTRYP	PORTLY	stout; fat
REEPPTSC	PRECEPTS	practical rules guiding conduct
YRIGIUSPOLOD	PRODIGIOUSLY	enormously; hugely
MEOPENRSCED	RECOMPENSED	repaid
CEUBRENTM	RECUMBENT	reclining; lying down
EERLSTN	RELENTS	softens in attitude or temper
DEOANRSTRTEM	REMONSTRATED	protested
ROUELTES	RESOLUTE	determined
DROIDS	SORDID	filthy; vile
PLATONICISUP	SUPPLICATION	asking for humbly or earnestly; praying
BUSCESTILEP	SUSCEPTIBLE	impressionable; easily influenced
BUUIUITOSQ	UBIQUITOUS	being everywhere
YNUNIMAIT	UNANIMITY	complete agreement